PAINLESS
Study
Techniques

Michael Greenberg, M.A.

Illustrations by Michele Earle-Bridges

About the Author
Michael Greenberg is the English Department Head at Great Neck North Middle School. He is the author of Barron's *Painless Vocabulary* and Barron's *New York State Grade 8 English Language Arts Test*.

Dedication
I would like to acknowledge the expertise of my colleagues at Great Neck North Middle School, whose ideas inform nearly every page of this book. And I would like to thank my mother and father, who impressed upon me the importance and satisfaction of studying.

All inquiries should be addressed to:
Barron's Educational Series, Inc.
250 Wireless Boulevard
Hauppauge, NY 11788
www.barronseduc.com

ISBN-13: 978-0-7641-4059-4
ISBN-10: 0-7641-4059-0

Library of Congress Catalog No.: 2008042609

Library of Congress Cataloging-in-Publication Data
Greenberg, Michael, 1951–
  Painless study techniques / Michael Greenberg.
    p. cm.
  Includes bibliographical references and index.
  ISBN-13: 978-0-7641-4059-4
  ISBN-10: 0-7641-4059-0
  1. Study Skills.   I. Title.

LB1049.G733 2009
371.3'0281—dc22   2008042609

Printed in China
9 8 7 6 5

CONTENTS

HOW TO USE THIS BOOK

You are holding this book in your hands for one reason and one reason only: your parent purchased it for you.

Just kidding! The real reason: you wish to become a better student.

Good for you! That is a commendable goal, and reading this book is a solid first step toward achieving it.

This book takes the approach that becoming a better student is the result of two distinctly different processes. The first of these is acquiring certain skills. As a result of reading this book, you will develop many skills you did not possess before. These will run from learning to maximize your time to reading different kinds of books to taking notes for different purposes to creating useful outlines—and on and on.

The second process involves developing habits. As you certainly know, habits can be harmful. You may not be thrilled that you bite your nails, your parents may wonder why you seem determined to leave your laundry (and everything else) on the bedroom floor, and your teacher may criticize you for doodling when the rest of class is taking careful notes. But habits can also be very useful. Observe the way a careful driver signals before changing lanes. Check out the way a skilled ballroom dancer gracefully glides along the dance floor. Think about the disaster your life would become if you didn't routinely set the alarm clock.

Whether habits are harmful or helpful, this much you know: habits can be hard to develop and hard to break. For sure, the ballroom dancer did not acquire that level of skill overnight. No way! That kind of performance requires hours, months, and years of practice until complex steps and difficult rhythms become second nature. On the other hand, ask any nail biter whether quitting the habit or moving mountains would be more challenging.

Don't be intimidated! In a way, this works in your favor. Once you develop excellent study habits, you will own them for a very long time—and you may even be able to apply them to areas outside the classroom.

Some effort will certainly be required, but remember that *effort* is not *pain*. Moreover, the rewards you will accrue will easily compensate you for the effort you have expended. And just in case you are less than 100 percent sure of that, remember how super you felt when you saw your report card and realized that the B you had earned in math last quarter had magically become an A.

CHAPTER ONE

You Can Manage Your Time

Andrew Marvell begins his famous poem, "To His Coy Mistress," with these lines:

> *Had we but world enough, and time,*
> *This coyness, Lady, were no crime.*

The narrator, faced with a hesitant mistress, tries to persuade her to love him, and this is his argument: let's get a move on, because we don't have forever. It is a classic statement of the principle of *carpe diem*, literally "seize the day."

So you are not the first person—nor will you be the last—to lament the fact that our time is finite. There are only so many years in a life span, so many days in any given year, and so many hours in any given day. Your responsibility is to use them well.

And now you've made a decision to use more of them to study.

YOUR TYPICAL DAY

Chances are you wake up earlier than you'd like to, and you get to sleep later than you should. Nevertheless, as you're brushing your teeth and donning your pajamas, you might mutter these words: "Boy, where did that day go?"

You need to answer that question.

The easiest way to do so is to chart your schedule for a week. Get your hands on a diary or a planner or just create a spreadsheet that includes the entire waking day in thirty-minute denominations. *Keep it with you all the time.* Only by doing so can you maintain an accurate record of how you use your time.

And be honest! And don't leave out any of the juicy details!

So maybe your first day looks something like this:

7:00	Wake up, get dressed, eat breakfast (oatmeal . . . again!)
8:00	Leave for school
8:20	School (the usual)
3:20	Basketball practice (guarded and was guarded by Derren . . . made him look silly)
5:00	Pizza with Steve and Jerzy
6:00	Home: change and shower

6:30	Play _Madden '07_
7:00	Social studies, math homework
7:30	Dinner
8:00	Watch ball game, do Spanish homework during commercials
9:00	Watch _24_ (this show is getting old)
10:00	Surf the net, watch end of ball game (PATRIOTS WIN!)
10:30	Reading _Great Expectations_, but start to fall asleep (no surprise there)
11:00	Wash up, go to sleep

Does this look familiar? Does your day look anything like this?

You get the idea, right? Go ahead then. Do it for a full week, and that includes the weekends. That's your assignment for the next seven days. Place a bookmark on this page, put the book down, and one week from now come back to it.

ONE WEEK LATER: TIME TO CONSIDER SOME SACRIFICES

So, how was your week?

Before you continue reading, you should have at your side a detailed record of how you spent the previous seven days. If you can, set aside for now the two sheets that chronicle your weekend; you'll examine your weekends a little later in this chapter.

So what patterns do you notice?

First of all, there's sleep. How much do you sleep on a typical school night? (By "school night," we mean those from Sunday through Thursday.) Total your sleep hours for these five nights, and divide by five. What's your average? Six hours? Seven? Eight? More?

BRAIN TICKLER
Set #1

Call a few friends. Ask them how much sleep they get. See when they get to bed and when they rise. See how your sleep schedule compares with theirs.

Are you ready for some good news? *Really* good news? Even though this sub-chapter heading makes reference to "some sacrifices," you will be relieved to learn that sleep is not one of them. This book will not ask you to hit the sack at 9:00 P.M., nor will it demand that you rise at 5:00 A.M. to begin studying.

In fact, experts are nearly unanimous in concluding that adolescents do not get enough sleep. You want to hear some interesting numbers? Well, check these out. Children (that is, ten years of age and younger) need ten hours of sleep. Adolescents (ages eleven through twenty-two) require nine hours and fifteen minutes of sleep.

Are you getting that much? Are your friends? Probably not. Experts report that 70 percent of teens suffer from sleep deprivation.

Here's what makes the problem especially hard to solve. At some point in adolescence, teens begin to secrete melatonin, a sleep-related hormone, at different hours. The result is a change in sleep patterns. Getting up at 7:00 A.M. seems like a Herculean task! Later, in the evening, when your parents are yawning and just beginning their struggle to stay awake, you feel as if you're just getting started: sleep is the last thing on your mind.

School officials, parents, and pediatricians have begun to understand that these sleep patterns cause lots of kids to have a hard time getting started in the morning. Little wonder! Sleep deprivation is a serious problem. Obviously, a sleep-deprived individual may experience some difficult focusing in class, but what's less obvious is that sleep deprivation can inhibit students' creativity. And there are medical consequences, too. Sleep deprivation can lower your resistance to illness, cause accidents, and even lead to depression.

Having taken note of these problems, some officials and parent groups have gone so far as to recommend a much later starting time for secondary schools. When Minnesota changed its high schools' starting time from 7:15 to 8:40, students began to earn higher grades. Who knows? Maybe one day you'll see a starting time of 9:30 or 10:00, but chances are right now your school gets under way a lot earlier than that.

So, once again, the good news: you're not going to have to sacrifice sleep. On the contrary, because you now understand that getting enough sleep will aid your growth as a student, you should try to sleep well. Here are some steps you can take:

- Stay away from caffeine. Caffeine is a stimulant that could affect your sleep. You might not know that the smaller the person, the greater the effect caffeine can have. If you drink any caffeine beverages, make sure you consume them prior to 12:00 noon. The same goes for foods rich in caffeine.
- Don't go to sleep with the TV or your bedroom lights on. Doctors suspect that teenagers develop an acute sensitivity to light, which might interfere with a good night's sleep.
- Avoid stressful situations in the hour or two before bedtime. Let's face it: it's not like you have absolute control over these things. However, to the extent that you can, try not to get into any prolonged shouting matches with your parents, siblings, or friends during the late evening hours.
- Use your last hour before sleep to wind down. It's not a good time for intense studying or for really exciting video games. Opt instead for something sedate, like reading a magazine or watching some low-key television program.

- Many teens, sleep deprived during the week, use the weekend for catch-up sleep. They think, with another week of school coming up, it's a good idea to store some sleep hours in the sleep bank, and to some extent, they're right. However, sleep experts say that you shouldn't sleep more than two hours more than you usually do. For example, if you've been getting seven hours of sleep during the school week, try not to get more than nine hours on the weekend. Experts claim that doing so can very badly throw off your sleep schedule.

So you don't have to sacrifice sleep. Painless indeed!

BRAIN TICKLER
Set #2
When you hear the word "caffeine," you probably think, "Coffee." However, other food products contain significant amounts of caffeine, too. Go online, and learn which common foods might interfere with your sleep.

Let's get back to those five-day school week schedules. You can't do anything about the block of time you spend in school. If you wake at 7:00, leave for school at 8:00, and finish with school at around 3:00, that's a block of eight used hours. Add to that the eight hours you sleep, and you can see that you have no room to tinker with at least two-thirds of a twenty-four-hour day.

So what's left?

Well, you have to eat, right? And your parents will probably insist that you join them for a family dinner that may take another hour out of your day.

Also, you may be someone who must allocate a certain amount of time after school to mandated activities. Perhaps you must attend religious school several hours a week. Maybe you

take private lessons of some sort—learning to play a musical instrument, for example. Some students have medical needs such as physical therapy that require several hours per week. Or maybe, to supplement your family's income or just to fatten your own wallet, you work an after-school job.

And that brings us to the subject of extracurricular activities. There is no shortage of activities you can choose if you want to get involved in something larger than yourself. Many schools field multiple sports teams in each of three or four cycles, and if you're not good enough for varsity or j.v., you can always settle for intramurals. If you like to write, you can work for the school's literary magazine, yearbook, or newspaper, and there's a good chance that other subjects offer their own publications, too. If you like math, there's the math team. If science is your thing, join the science Olympiad. Are you into debating? How about chess? Yoga? Photography? Did anyone mention music? Let's not forget about the chorus, glee club, band, or orchestra. Do you like plays? Well, you can act or dance in one or become a member of the backstage crew that pulls the whole show together. And don't most schools sponsor clubs for various ethnic groups?

Student government, anyone? You have to admire those aspiring politicians.

And here's the really cool part: if you're an enthusiast of some relatively obscure activity for which your school does not presently have a club, all you have to do is find a few like-minded enthusiasts and a faculty adviser, and you're in business.

BRAIN TICKLER
Set #3

Most schools hold club fairs in the beginning of the school year in order to inform students of the variety of clubs they may join. At the same time, school officials produce a list of clubs. This list contains the names of faculty advisers and meeting times and places. Go to the office (or to the student government adviser) and ask for such a list. Or check out your school's website. Which activities does your school offer that this chapter has failed to mention? Which activities are "news" to you?

Students join clubs and participate in school activities for a number of very good reasons. They have interests they wish to pursue and skills they wish to develop. Sometimes, especially in high schools, students participate in extracurricular activities because it looks good on a college application or resume.

But the underlying reason for joining just about all school activities is this: it's nice to make connections with other people. Meeting new people is fun, and it's easy if you share interests. It can be especially exciting to befriend people who are not in your immediate social circle, people who might be different from you in one way or another. After all, anyone can go straight home and stare at the TV or a computer monitor, but spending time with your peers sure beats loneliness and isolation.

Major Mistake Territory!

Have you ever heard of the Golden Mean? That's a term people use to express a familiar idea: you can get too much of a good thing. Yes, participating in extracurricular activities is a very good thing, but some people don't know where to draw the line. The result? Joining too many clubs can sap large chunks of your free time.

22 Monday
Math extra help 3:15
play practice 3:45
ballet lesson 5:00
baby sitting @ 7:30

23 Tuesday
band practice 3:15

This is especially true during certain crunch times. If you work for a school newspaper and your deadline is approaching, you know that you might have to spend evenings and even weekends making sure the paper is as perfect as you want it to be. Anyone who has ever been associated with a school play knows how all-consuming that activity becomes as the play's opening nears.

Pacing is important. Some activities, like sports, require intense, nearly daily participation for two or three months, but then you're done. Another activity, such as a photography club, will probably meet once a week throughout the year. Keep in mind, too, that you might be taking a particularly challenging course that requires extra research or study. Some students must set aside large amounts of time to prepare for personal, religious, or family obligations.

The point is this: if you don't exercise some moderation in terms of your extracurricular activities, you can become awfully stressed out about the tasks you absolutely need to complete, such as studying. That's a situation you must avoid. So get involved in those activities that are most meaningful to you, and make sure you don't overextend yourself. If you explain such a problem to a club's faculty adviser, he or she will surely understand your predicament and excuse you from that activity.

At this point, you might be thinking, "I don't have to give up sleep or a leisurely dinner with my family, and it's OK for me to participate in extracurricular activities. So where's the sacrifice?"

That's easy. Turn back to that sample schedule on pages 3–4. You're going to notice that there's a chunk of time—or, more accurately, several chunks of time—that could be used more constructively. As you scan that schedule and your own, you will see that certain fun activities can be reduced or eliminated.

Here, at last, is the sacrifice. You're going to have to spend less time online, surfing the net, or instant messaging your friends. You're going to have to spend less time on your phone—and that includes text messages. You're going to have to give up some of the time you spend playing video games. You're going to have to watch less TV.

Look, no one is going to deny that these activities are fun, and you don't have to give them up entirely. But you have a goal—you want to clear some more time for studying because you are determined to become a better student.

Here are some strategies that will make the sacrifice less painful:

1. Reward yourself for time spent studying. Make a deal with yourself: "If I study for, say, thirty minutes, I can spend fifteen minutes on my Xbox." That's fair. You deserve a reward. (But make sure you keep to that fifteen minutes!)

2. Set aside some downtime just before you go to bed. As we said earlier, doing this will help you get to sleep. This is an excellent time to watch some TV, answer emails, or perform some other low-key activity.

3. Set realistic goals for yourself. If you are now spending thirty minutes a night on schoolwork, it's just not realistic to expect yourself to jump to two hours per night. Settle on some incremental improvement. Even a little bit of extra time and effort will yield results.

4. Brag. Look, there's nothing wrong with letting your parents know that you've been spending more time on your schoolwork. After all, if you were spending less time, they would certainly let you know! So bring this to their attention. Brag a little bit. Curry some good favor.

BRAIN TICKLER
Set #4

It's time for a little math. Do you have your calculator handy?

Let's say you study fifteen minutes more per night. Over the course of a single school year (forty weeks, six days a week—go ahead and take a day off), how many additional hours of studying will you do?

What happens if you go thirty minutes extra?

USING TIME IN SCHOOL

One very simple way to free up some time in the evening is to use your time in school more productively. Here are some measures you can take that will make a difference in your evening workload:

1. Organize! If you are already an organized person, it's a skill you probably take for granted. If you're not, there may be no greater mystery than how to become one. Chapter 2 offers some concrete suggestions about organizing yourself for school. These include maintaining a notebook, recording your assignments, and finding the materials you'll need. By organizing yourself and your possessions, you avoid wasting valuable time. So pay close attention!

2. Be punctual. Have you ever wondered why some students arrive early to school nearly every day, while others habitually arrive late? To which group do you belong, and why? Arriving early to school has huge time-saving advantages. For one thing, it's a great time to hit the library or the computer center. For another, you have a chance to meet with teachers for extra help sessions. Also, there's lots of essential socializing that's conducted before the homeroom bell, so you might get that out of your system. And it's just as important to arrive at class on time. Teachers

like to start class just when the bell rings, and you don't want to miss any information dispensed at that time.

3. Take advantage of free time. If you have a study hall, you may have the choice of deciding whether to use that time to chat with your friends or to get some homework or studying done. The same is true if a teacher is absent. Most teachers routinely leave absentee plans, but those activities rarely take a full period. Sometimes kids explain to their parents, "I did most of my homework in school," and often parents don't believe them, but you probably know how much work you can actually complete in a quiet forty-minute study hall.

MAJOR MISTAKE TERRITORY!

School districts report that, on a typical day, 8 to 12 percent of students are absent. Some students are obviously absent more than others, but occasionally practically everyone needs to miss a day. If you must miss a day of school, don't compound the problem by thinking of it as a "day off"—a small taste of early summer vacation! If you do, you will find that catching up to your classmates can be a very stressful experience.

Therefore, do your best to find out what work you've missed. Call your classmates, check your teachers' websites, and review the test and homework schedules you've been given. Complete whatever work you can. Because you missed instruction or do not have in your possession the necessary materials, there is a very good chance that you will not be able to complete everything. Do what you can; it will make your return to school that much easier.

Of course, if you are so ill that doing schoolwork is simply not an option, don't worry about it. Your first obligation is getting better.

WEEKENDS AND HOLIDAYS

Remember those two sheets you set aside? The ones on which you recorded your weekend schedules? Take them out now, and let's look them over.

If you're like most teenagers, your weekend schedule probably demonstrates some of these characteristics:

- You sleep a whole lot! On Friday and Saturday nights, you get to sleep somewhat later than usual, and the following mornings you rise much, much later than usual. You have a pair of simple explanations for this. First, you have not gotten enough sleep during the school week, and now you need to catch up. Second, looking ahead to another sleep-deprived week, you know that you've got to store some sleep hours in the sleep bank.

- You seriously hang out with your friends. Oh, you've seen your friends (or most of them) during the week—at school, at soccer practice, at Luigi's Pizzeria—but that's not serious hanging out; that's interrupted hanging out. You are interrupted by the bell that ends lunch, the coach's whistle that sends you to your next drill, and your mother who is parked outside, honking, reminding you in her subtle way that you're not the only person for whom she's responsible. Now it's the weekend, and you're ready for a slab of hanging out time—a movie, an afternoon at the mall, maybe someone's birthday party.

- We're talking about lots of down time: emails and IMs that need to be read and sent, TV shows that you've TiVoed, a veritable tournament of video thrills . . . whatever floats your boat.

- Bad news! You have some obligation that will devour three or four of the precious hours you were planning to allocate to sleep/hanging out/downtime. Maybe your family insists you accompany them on the visit to grandmother's house. Maybe you have a babysitting job that will knock out Saturday night. Even if you don't mind this activity, you resent the fact that it will cut into your plans for continuous weekend pleasure.

- Dinner on Sunday offers a painful reminder that the weekend is drawing to a close, that at one point in the not-too-distant past you were a student attending a school, that within a few short hours you will be a student once again. In other words, forty-eight hours have passed, and you haven't done a single thing for school. You have homework due in science, French, and English, and a test in social studies. You hope dessert will last forever because you don't want to get started.

Is this an accurate depiction of your weekend? Well, if so, here's some good news: there is another way, and, as the saying goes, you can have your cake and eat it.

First of all, take a day off. Maybe you'd prefer Friday, since you simply need to get your weekend started—and that means nothing to do with school once that dismissal bell rings at 3:00. Maybe you'd like to take off Saturday because you relish the thought of one huge, delicious twenty-four-hour block of school-less life. Or maybe Sunday's your day off because you crave the idea of football, football, and a little more football. Go with whatever works for you, and try to be consistent about which day you select. Remember: you're building good habits.

Second, take advantage of the flexibility that weekends and vacations offer. During the school week, you may not be free to begin your homework and studying until after dinner. But weekends and vacations allow you to study just about whenever you like. Maybe, for example, you're a morning person (relatively speaking, of course: you are a teenager, after all!). If so, try to get most of your schoolwork done before lunch. Your friends aren't up to keep you company, anyway, and this way you can clear the day.

Third, plan ahead. When you begin to have a pretty good sense of your weekend requirements—both academic and social—you can carve out a schedule for yourself. But it's essential that you take a few minutes to do this. You may know by Friday that you're going with your friends to the movies on Friday night, working in your parents' store on Saturday afternoon, and attending Sunday school at your house of worship. At the same time, you may also realize that you need to complete a journal entry for English, knock off two worksheets for Spanish, read and answer some questions for social studies, complete a lab report for earth science, and begin studying for a World War II unit test on Wednesday. That's a lot of work for one weekend, and you'll need a plan of attack. Create one as soon as you can, and stick to it.

Finally, work in manageable chunks of time. The weekend gives you more than forty-eight hours to complete your work, and vacations give you a lot more time. That means, even with your taking a day off, you still have multiple opportunities to get your schoolwork done. If you have a workload like the one described above, you might schedule your study time this way:

> Friday: my day off (yippee!)
>
> Saturday
> • 10:00–11:00 Read/write journal entry
> • 4:00–5:00 Do social studies homework
>
> Sunday
> • 11:00–11:30 Complete Spanish worksheets/finish earth science lab
> • 7:00–8:00 Begin studying for Wednesday's test

That's not bad. You're studying for three and a half hours, but never for more than one hour at a time. A tedious chore will seem a lot less tedious if you do it in manageable chunks. And you still have lots of time for weekend rest and relaxation.

Major Mistake Territory!

Vacations are great, but don't let your vacation become a time when you abandon the good habits you've worked so hard to develop. And don't let it be a time when you allow yourself to fall behind in school.

First of all, try not to take vacations when school is in session. Of course, you don't always have control over the

timing of vacations, but you might have some input. Your parents won't mind hearing that you'd rather not miss too much school. And, if you must miss school, be sure to talk to your teachers about getting some assignments beforehand.

Second, try to get some work accomplished. Take some of your books with you, and try to contact your teachers' Web sites to get a sense of what's been going on while you're away. Whatever you can accomplish on vacation means less work to make up once you get back. Again, do your best to keep some routine, whether it's setting aside some studying time first thing in the morning or getting some reading done poolside.

Third, plane flights and layovers can be ridiculously long, so take some work with you.

Finally, as soon as you get home, find out from your teachers and your classmates exactly what you've missed. Create a schedule that will enable you to catch up in a timely manner.

GROUP PROJECTS

Some teachers are especially fond of assigning group projects, while others will hardly assign them at all. For teachers the problem with group assignments is fairness: they are hard to grade. A group grade will not take into account the different contributions made by different students. If a group presents only a group project, it may be impossible to determine individual contributions and assign individual grades.

Teachers give a lot of careful thought to the composition of groups. In most cases, they assemble groups that are heterogeneous in nature. They try to include a representative mix of students. If you have spent any time in groups, you know what usually happens: the best students end up doing much of the work, while the weaker students contribute far less.

BRAIN TICKLER
Set #5

Consider your own role in group projects.
Answer these questions honestly.

1. Do you assume a leadership role in groups?
   How do you know?

2. Do you play a major role in organizing the
   group's effort? Give an example of
   something you've done to help the group
   get or stay on track.

3. Do you contribute your fair share of the
   work? (In other words, do you provide
   more than what is required, exactly what is
   required, or less than what is required?)

4. Do you think most of your classmates are
   pleased to discover that you are in their
   group?

This chapter's emphasis is on using time effectively, not on
improving your response to group challenges. However, if you
improve your own productivity and exercise some leadership,
you can help your group to use time effectively. Here are some
concrete contributions you can make:

1. Help decide upon a realistic meeting time and place.
   People's lives are complex. They are subject to all sorts of
   constraints. This is a good time to be flexible and to help
   others be so, too.

2. Help the group determine an end time. Group tasks often
   take longer than people anticipate.

3. Arrive on time. Make sure you are well-prepared: that means
   you have completed the tasks for which you are responsible.
   Encourage the group to start promptly.

4. Stick to the agenda. Stay focused, and politely help others to keep focused, too. Keep extraneous conversations to a minimum. Don't let the group's precious time be spent on a long conversation about what to order for lunch.

5. Before the group disperses, establish an agenda, time, and place for your next meeting. Make sure everyone knows what his or her responsibilities are.

If you can perform these time-saving tasks and help others do so, you are demonstrating leadership. That's an interesting way to think of leadership: helping others to use time productively.

Getting Some Organization Assistance

In order to use your time more efficiently, you must take steps to get yourself organized. To this end, certain products can be very helpful. Here are just a few:

1. Use your own alarm clock. In other words, don't depend on someone else to get you started in the morning. Do you know how feeble it sounds when a student blames his lateness on a parent? That's almost as bad as "the dog ate my homework." That's a situation you want to avoid.

2. Buy a planner. This is absolutely essential. Your planner will be your guide to everything having to do with school. Here you will record all information pertaining to homework assignments and upcoming tests and quizzes. (Of course, you can use it for out-of-school activities, too.) If you lose your planner (hey, it's been known to happen), replace it as quickly as possible.

3. Make use of hi-tech planning devices. Computers and cell phones offer easy-to-use schedule and planning programs. These can help remind you of important upcoming events and commitments. There's nothing wrong with leaving yourself an electronic reminder!

Above all, if you're really determined to make more efficient use of time, simply stop and ask yourself what you need to accomplish. And don't waste time because it won't come again.

BRAIN TICKLERS
THE ANSWERS

Set #1, page 5

Answers will vary.

Set #2, page 7

Caffeine is present in coffee, but it can also be found in tea, chocolate (and chocolate products), soft drinks, pain relievers, and alertness pills. In fact, caffeine is the active ingredient in many pick-me-up products. So be careful: the lift you get in the morning could come back to haunt you when you're trying to fall asleep.

Set #3, page 9

Answers will vary.

Set #4, page 12

Fifteen extra minutes will yield exactly thirty-six extra hours of studying. Thirty minutes extra will give you seventy-two hours.

Set #5, page 18

Answers will vary.

CHAPTER TWO

Homework:
Practically a Misnomer

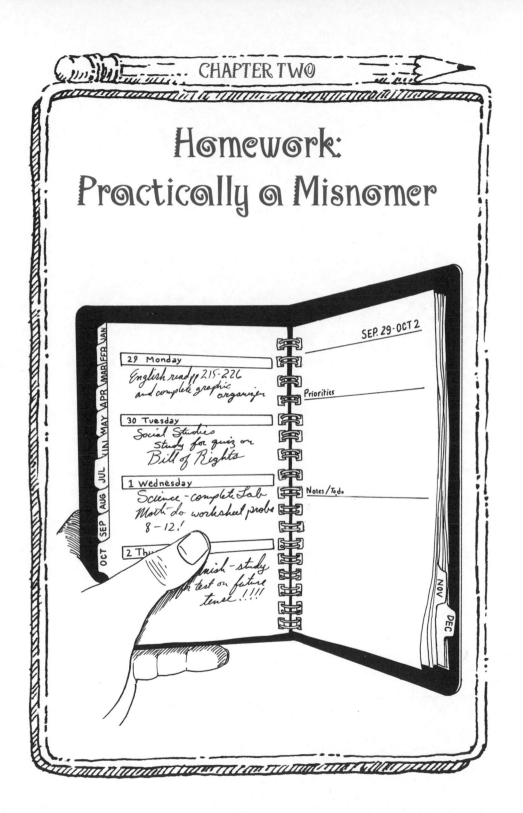

Imagine you are asking someone to free associate, in this case to utter the first thing that comes to mind when that person hears the word "school." There's a very good chance that the response would be "homework."

The idea of homework is so closely associated with elementary and secondary education for a very good reason: it has long been a part of practically everyone's school experience. And you can take it a step further: it has probably been seen as a profoundly *negative* part of that experience.

No one likes homework. Homework has a bad rep.

But this chapter suggests that the very term *homework* is practically a misnomer: it has, to an extent, been wrongly named. Why? That's simple. One reason: much of the actual work pertaining to homework must be done in school. Another reason: if properly managed, homework need not become the bane of your existence.

THE REASON FOR HOMEWORK

Teachers do not assign homework merely to torment school-age children. Although some schools and some departments enforce minimum homework requirements, teachers assign homework for valid educational purposes. Here are some of these:

- Homework assignments help students review and practice the skills and concepts learned in class.
- Homework assignments permit students to apply their knowledge and skills to new arenas.
- Homework assignments prepare students for the next day's instruction.

You will not find on this list such sinister objectives as "to interfere with one's TV watching," or "to keep a kid from spending quality time with his friends," or "to bore a teenager to tears." Your teachers' motives are, after all, humane. Remember that when you're struggling to complete an assignment!

BRAIN TICKLER
Set #6

Go online and try to get some information about the average amount of homework assigned. See if you can find out about the "ten minute rule." How does this average compare with the amount of homework you typically receive?

Most of the news about homework will not lift your spirits. A couple of recent studies have confirmed that students spend about 50 percent more time on homework than they did in 1981. That means that a 1981 ninth grader who spent two hours a night on homework would be setting aside a third hour in 2008. (Of course, that's a very long time to remain in the ninth grade!) And, while studies show that more time spent on homework generally means higher grades, here too one can have too much of a good thing: middle and high school students who take more than two hours to complete homework do not earn higher grades than their classmates who study more moderately.

The growing time requirement is not the only problem, critics say. They also contend that homework is often dull and unimaginative. It ends up stifling creativity and lowering students' enthusiasm toward school and learning.

Some critics argue that the time can be spent more productively. Students can participate in extracurricular activities in and out of school, perform community service, or work. Or maybe a kid can read a book just for fun.

And there are many people who will now admit that activities such as playing video games and watching TV, once considered wasteful, are challenging and educational.

As a result, some schools have adopted policies that place a limit on homework. Perhaps your school will adopt such a policy. (You can only hope!) But until that time, you need to bring a positive approach to dealing with these demands.

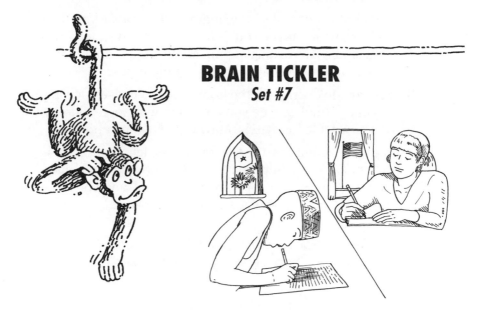

BRAIN TICKLER
Set #7

Certainly not everyone agrees that American schools are assigning too much homework. Some feel that America's children lag behind those of other countries because they spend less time on homework.

Go online and see what you can learn about this issue. Do Americans do less homework than the children of other countries?

The Dog Didn't Eat Your Homework

Naturally the dog didn't eat it, and chances are your printer's ink cartridge didn't suddenly run dry either. These time-tested (and completely transparent) excuses serve only to camouflage the real reasons homework is not done—or done well.

The following reasons will probably sound a little more realistic:

1. You couldn't complete your homework because of some organizational problem: you didn't have the assignment, you didn't have the necessary textbook, or you didn't have the required handouts.

2. You couldn't complete the homework because you didn't understand it. Maybe you didn't understand exactly what the assignment was asking of you. Maybe you didn't understand exactly how to complete the assignment.

3. You couldn't complete the homework because you simply ran out of time. Maybe you have overextended yourself with extracurricular activities. Maybe you planned poorly.

4. You didn't complete the homework assignment because you didn't consider it important. You had other, easier, more amusing options for spending an evening, and you selected those instead of completing your homework.

Do these reasons sound familiar? If you haven't experienced them yourself, you have certainly heard them emerge from the mouths of others.

PREPARATION: WHAT YOU MUST DO AT SCHOOL

It's not as if there's some huge wall that magically divides school and home. On the contrary, what happens in one place has a huge impact on what might happen in the other. You know that if you fail to complete your homework, you will probably not enjoy the following day of school. By the same token, your efforts in school will largely determine your attitude toward and competence in homework.

Of paramount importance is your classroom performance. What kind of student are you? How would your teachers describe your classroom behavior? How would you rate yourself?

BRAIN TICKLER
Set #8

Rate your classroom performance. Think of a typical day and a typical period. Check the box that applies to you.

	Most of the Time	Sometimes	Rarely
I arrive punctually.			
I have with me all the supplies and books I need.			
I pay attention to the teacher and the lesson.			
I do my best to complete all classroom activities.			
I ask questions when I'm unsure about what is being taught.			
I participate in classroom discussions.			

Consider too the question of consistency: does this rating apply to all classes, or do you take some classes—and subjects—more seriously than others? Does your performance vary according to the time of day? Are you sluggish in the morning? Are you "wired" after you've eaten a carbohydrate-laden lunch? Are you a little feisty as the day draws to a close and you eagerly anticipate dismissal?

In any case, you know yourself, and, if you've been honest in the Brain Tickler above, then you know where you have to improve. Remember that the main goal of homework is to review what is taught in school. If you didn't get it then, you probably won't get it in the cozy confines of your own home.

Major Mistake Territory!

Teenagers are social. Most enjoy the company of their peers and give a great deal of thought to important social issues. Consequently, for some teenagers, striking a reasonable balance between academics and friends can be very hard.

But if you're really concerned about improving your academic performance, you might have to do the un-cool thing. You might have to refrain from answering a classmate who is whispering to you. You might have to let a neighbor in your science class know that you are not interested in passing notes. You might even have to ask your teacher to change your seat because it's hard for you to stay focused in your present one.

Go for it! Risk it! No one's approval matters more than your own.

If classroom performance is primary, then let's call organization "almost primary," because that's how important it is. Organization at school will abet production at home. Chapter 1 offered some suggestions about saving time, but some of these time-saving suggestions really hinge upon your ability to get yourself organized.

1. Maintain an orderly book bag. Does yours look like a neat library shelf, or does it more closely resemble the town

dump? Do you have in it everything you need: textbooks, looseleaf paper, notebooks, pens and pencils, calculator, erasers, cell phones, money, house keys, gum, lip balm . . . did we leave anything out? Moreover, do you know where to find everything? When was the last time you cleaned it out? Here's what you need to do: every couple of weeks, go through your bag and make sure you have only the items you need. Mark it down on your planner.

2. Maintain orderly notebooks. Keep sections for each subject. (Some subject teachers will ask you to keep multiple sections.) Make sure you go through it so that you have only the papers you actually need. A good time to do this is the end of a marking period. If you're not sure whether something can be discarded, ask your teacher.

3. Maintain an orderly locker. Some people put a great deal of energy and creativity into keeping attractive, personalized, well-ordered lockers. Others pretend that a locker is simply a vertical bedroom floor, in other words, a perfect place to chuck anything and everything. (At the end of the year, stand by as a student cleans out his or her locker. You will hear these words as the student eventually finds his or her way to the bottom: "So *that's* where that sweatshirt went!") If you want some excellent advice in terms of caring for this space, take some measurements and visit a container store. For a small sum of money, you can purchase some excellent storage organizers.

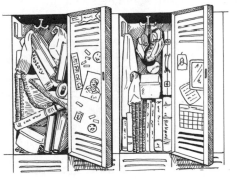

4. Record your assignments carefully and completely. First of all, where do you write your assignments? Do you have an assignment pad? If you don't, you should. Is your name written on it in case it's misplaced? Most teachers write the homework on the board at the very beginning of the period, and classes often begin with the teacher's reminding you to copy it down. Do that—and do it neatly. If you have any questions about the homework, ask them then or at any time during the period. Knowing exactly what you will need to do will save you lots of time that might otherwise be spent calling your friends to get the assignments.

5. Before you leave school, check your assignment pad, and make sure you have everything you will need for homework and studying: textbooks, workbooks, handouts . . . whatever. Yes, stand there in front your locker, and, even if you look like a complete nerd, review every assignment, and make sure you have whatever you need. Once you get home and discover that you've left your science workbook in school, it's too late to do anything about it. So organize yourself before you get on the bus.

In addition to organizing yourself and your possessions, you can make really good use of your school's facilities and programs. Does your school have a homework help center? Many schools run after-school homework help centers, which are staffed by teachers or teacher aides. Here you are guaranteed a quiet work environment in which to complete at least some of your homework. If finding such an environment at home is hard for you, you would be wise to take advantage of this opportunity.

Seek extra help. Teachers work hard, and they love to see their students succeed. Most teachers derive special satisfaction from seeing a student make the extra effort. For this reason,

teachers routinely offer extra help sessions to individuals or small groups. Extra help may be available before the start of classes, during lunch, or after school. Some teachers establish a regular extra help schedule; most will see students by appointment, which probably means that you will need to get a pass beforehand. If there's something going on in class that you don't understand, go for extra help. Chances are your homework and the next test for which you must study will be based on this same material. You don't want to arrive home and have to deal with material you just don't understand. At that hour it's going to be hard to find someone who can help you. Extra help is an amazing opportunity for you to get one-on-one assistance from someone who knows exactly what you need to learn. Take advantage!

A WORKING ENVIRONMENT

When you're a highly successful adult, rising meteorically to the very top of your field, perhaps you will buy a house or apartment with a separate study. You know the kind that you see in movies and on TV: floor-to-ceiling bookcases, a luxurious leather couch, a really spacious desk with a cool swivel chair, a large flat-screen computer monitor perched on your desk, and lush wall-to-wall carpeting.

Until then you might have to settle for something more modest.

Along those lines, let's consider the essential ingredients for your homework environment:

- You need privacy so that you can concentrate on your work. Not everyone has his or her own bedroom, which of course would ensure privacy, so you may have to be resourceful in effecting some other arrangement. Maybe you will decide to alternate homework/ study times with your sibling: the bedroom is yours from 7:30 to 8:30, his from 8:30 to 9:30. Maybe you can take over the kitchen table after dinner. Maybe the living room is quiet in the afternoons. If possible, close the door.

- You must have with you all the materials you will need. If you are fortunate enough to have your own bedroom, this will not be a problem. If not, you will need to organize yourself before you get started. If you require access to a computer and your family has only one, you might have to be flexible about timing. That's not easy—not with your sister swapping emails, your mom checking the political blogs, and your dad arranging fantasy football trades. You will all have to work together, which means recognizing that schoolwork comes first.

- You must have sufficient light and, if possible, fresh air. If you're working at night, choose a space that has good lighting. Otherwise, your eyes—and the rest of you, for that matter—will grow weary.
- Avoid distractions and interruptions. This can be very difficult because some teens actually *welcome* distractions and interruptions. However, if you're going to get serious about homework and studying, you have to make some choices. That means the TV is off, you're not listening to music, you're not answering your cell phone, and your computer speakers are turned off, too (there can be no "You've got mail!" in the background!). Look, you know what distractions and interruptions can do: they make it hard for you to concentrate, and they stretch your homework/study time.

Does this describe your current workplace ambience? Which requirements do you meet? Where do you fall short?

Major Mistake Territory!

Here's a scene from forty years ago: a teenager is doing her homework, while a nearby transistor radio blasts Beatles tunes. A parent enters the room and barks, "Turn that thing off!" The teenager plaintively replies, "But it relaxes me. It helps me concentrate."

The technology and the music have certainly changed, but the argument remains the same. The simple truth is, you need to know yourself and what works for you. Some students can work well with music playing in the background; for others, the music is too much of a distraction and interferes with concentration.

One thing's for sure, however: television-watching is a no-no. Sorry about that, but it's true. Research shows that the longer the television is on, the less actual time is spent on homework. Apparently, the combination of image and sound is more distracting than sound alone.

TIME AND SEQUENCE

Here's the ideal situation: a student has a certain amount of homework—let's say two hours' worth—she comes home from school, retreats to her bedroom, works continuously for a couple of hours, and knocks off the whole thing by 6:00. Done. She not only has an hour before dinner; she's got the whole evening absolutely free and clear.

You know how good it feels when you complete a required task. If you've done your job well, you're especially satisfied. And you also know that if you delay a task, or if you let it drag on and on, it just becomes more of an annoyance. You're less likely to get it done. On top of that, you're not very pleased with yourself.

You know the ideal situation, but you also know that several factors may keep your situation from being ideal. First, after-school activities may delay your return home. Second, once you get home, you may have to confront other requirements, such as chores or dinner with the family. Third, you may not possess the stamina to work that long without interruptions.

Here are some guidelines that will help you complete your homework in a timely manner:

1. Start as soon as you can. That doesn't mean you burst through the front door and make a bee-line to your room. Maybe you need to chat first with your brother. Maybe you need a snack. Maybe you have to check your emails. Do what you need to do, but don't let it take too long.

2. Organize yourself. Check your homework pad and consider other studying you may need to do. Set up a schedule for yourself.

3. Pay particular attention to sequence. If you can, keep to this very effective principle: easy-hard-easy. In other words, begin with a task you can knock off quickly and easily, then transition into your most challenging task, and finally round off the homework session with another relatively easy task. This way, you're getting off to a satisfying and successful start. While you're still fresh, you follow that with your toughest assignment. Then, while your stamina is waning, you end the session with another less challenging, yet successful, task.

4. Take small breaks when you need them. You know that sometimes you tire and your concentration wanders. You try to continue your work, but you're just not into it. Take a break, but not too long—just enough to refresh yourself.

5. Don't save your least favorite work for last. Talk about major mistakes! You know what happens. It's 10:00. You've been postponing the two chapters you must read in Thomas Hardy's *The Return of the Native*, but you can't postpone it any longer. You recline on your bed, and within five minutes, your lids turn impossibly heavy, the book slips from your hands . . . and the assignment remains undone. It's essential that you get this kind of task done earlier. Use the easy-hard-easy formula mentioned above.

BRAIN TICKLER
Set #9

Let's take a few minutes to reflect on some matters pertaining to homework sequence. Answer the following questions, focusing solely on your "major" subjects, those in which you're likely to receive homework assignments.

- What is your favorite subject? Why? Is it because you like the subject matter? Are you especially fond of the teacher? Are you doing well in this class? Is the homework interesting and varied?
- What is your least favorite subject? Why? Do you dislike the subject matter? Do you dislike the teacher? Are you doing poorly in the class? Is the homework tedious or excessive?
- What is your customary order for study and/or homework? How does this sequence connect to your responses to the preceding two questions?
- Based on your understanding of the easy-hard-easy principle, how will you revise your sequence of homework?

THE QUESTION OF QUALITY

"If a thing is worth doing, it is worth doing well."

That's one way of looking at the homework question.

Here is another:

"It's getting late, I'm tired, and I'd really like to watch *The Bachelor*. Mr. Stone, my French teacher, generally just looks to see if the homework is done—it's not like he reads every word and assigns a grade—so let me get this over with as quickly as I can, and we'll call it a night."

Big difference, right?

The truth of the matter is this: in the short run, it might not make much of a difference. Hey, there's some chance Mr. Stone won't check the homework at all, in which case you might tell yourself that you did it for nothing.

But remember these two simple facts. The first: you're doing your homework for yourself, not for Mr. Stone, because you want to become a better student. The second: you are concerned now not with the consequences of a single evening's effort, but with developing habits that will last you for years and years.

So you've made the decision to hand in really good work. What exactly does that mean?

Let's say your English teacher has given you this poem by Robert Frost. It's called "Dust of Snow." Your assignment is to read the poem carefully and to write a good paragraph about the poem's message.

The way a crow
Shook down on me
The dust of snow
From a hemlock tree

Has given my heart
A change of mood
And saved some part
Of a day I had rued.

Let's take a look at the first of two possible responses:

Frost's poem is mostly about the way he feels about having some snow fall on him. You would think he might find this somewhat annoying, and he does.

Here is the second response:

Robert Frost's poem, "A Dust of Snow," shows how a little event can make a big difference in a person's day. In this poem, that simple event occurs when a crow shakes some snow onto the narrator. It doesn't seem like much. It's the sort of thing a person could easily overlook. But it changes the narrator's mood and, even stronger, "saved some part/ Of a day I had rued."

Look at the two responses. The first is shorter, but that's not the only difference. The second includes in its topic sentence the title of the poem, and it supplies much more in the way of supporting details. It also happens to be correct, whereas the first is not. The poem's narrator enjoys the "dust of snow"; he does not find it annoying. Why did the second writer know this? Perhaps he discovered it because he bothered to look up the word *rue*. Having learned that *to rue* means to regret bitterly, he understood that the narrator's day had actually been a dismal one . . . until that snow fell on him.

Here's another example. Let's say you've been learning in your science class about the scientific method. You've discussed in class the various elements of the scientific method: the problem, the hypothesis, the experiment, the data, and the conclusion. Your science teacher has asked you to consider this question for homework: Why must a scientific experiment have only one variable?

This is a sensible question because it really addresses the very essence of the scientific method. You think you understand it pretty well, but just to make sure you look again at your classroom notes. Here is one answer you might produce:

A scientific experiment can have only one variable because you can be testing only one thing at a time.

Or you might take a more thorough approach:

> *In a scientific experiment, a variable is the factor that is being tested. A scientific experiment can have only one variable. The reason for this is simple. When you get your data, you need to be able to figure out which factor is responsible. If you have more than one variable, it will be impossible to determine which one is responsible for the results. For example, if you want to figure out the effect of sunlight on plant growth, the only variable in the experiment must be sunlight. If you create an experiment with other variables, such as heat or moisture, then you cannot know which one is responsible for differences in plant growth.*

What does the second answer do that the first does not? It's more than just length. For one thing, it begins by offering a definition of *variable*. Then this particular answer explains quite thoroughly and clearly the reason there can only be one variable. Finally, it offers an excellent example.

Are you ready to try one on your own?

BRAIN TICKLER
Set #10

Get your hands on any American history textbook (or feel free to use the Internet). Do a good job in answering this question: "Who was Nat Turner? Why weren't there more people like him?"

Quality work is correct, thorough, and detailed. Substance certainly matters.

So does style. Quality work *looks* good, too. Don't forget about that. There's something to be said for presentation. Write neatly, and if you don't have a legible handwriting, try to type your work. Some crossing out is OK, but you don't want to hand in work that is thick with ink stains. Hand in a neat sheet of paper, too. You shouldn't submit homework that looks like it joined you in the shower!

Remember that your work is a representation of who you are. When you write your name on the top of the paper, you're inviting people to make judgments about you. This is true not only in school, but also in your social life and later on when you enter the world of work.

IF YOU'RE HAVING TROUBLE

Sometimes you might get home, take out your homework, and discover that you cannot complete the assignment. Maybe you don't have everything you need, maybe you don't quite understand the directions, or maybe you simply don't know how to answer a question. This can be a very frustrating experience. It can certainly put a crimp in your plans.

The most important thing to remember is this: don't panic. There are some very concrete steps you can take to address the problem. Do the best that you can do to complete your work. Do not obsess over the single task you cannot complete. Don't let one assignment keep you from completing your other work.

Here are some of those steps:

1. Call a classmate. At the very beginning of the school year, make sure you get the phone numbers of a few responsible classmates. (Some teachers will insist that you do this.) Ask this person to help you solve your problem. Let's say you don't have the handout distributed in class that day. Perhaps your classmate can fax you a copy. If this person cannot help you, call one or two more.

2. Contact your teacher. Many teachers maintain homework Web sites, some of which afford students the chance to contact their teachers directly. For that matter, some teachers furnish their students with their e-mail addresses so that students can get just this kind of last-minute help. Take advantage of their professionalism and generosity.

3. Use a homework help Web site. These have become very popular options for students who need some assistance. Some schools and school districts actually have their own homework help Web sites. Perhaps you already know of one or two, or your friends could offer some recommendations. In any case, just use your search engine. Enter "homework" or "homework help," and your search engine will supply you with lots of potential sources of help. Some will connect you with real teachers and professional tutors.

4. Ask a family member. This option might not work for everyone. If you have an older sibling, he or she might be too busy with his or her own schoolwork. Your parents may also be busy. And there's a good chance that they cannot help you with your schoolwork. They probably studied these subjects many years ago and no longer remember them. (Ask your parent to recite the quadratic equation, for example.) Keep in mind, too, that curricula change over time.

Major Mistake Territory!

There's another reason not to involve your parents in your homework. Let's face it: most teens are quite eager to have their parents *less* involved in their schoolwork. Asking a parent to help invites their involvement and could open the door to unwanted conflict. "Why weren't you paying attention in class when the teacher was going over this material?" "Why didn't you ask a question if you didn't understand?" You don't feel like getting into it with your parents, especially when you have work you need to complete.

The bottom line: you know best the nature of your relationship with your siblings and parents. Some will be only too happy to help and may provide superb assistance. That's not always the case, however, so proceed with caution!

5. Use a professional tutor. Some families have the financial resources to hire a professional tutor; many do not. If you can avail yourself of this kind of service, you are lucky to have someone who provides highly qualified assistance. The potential problem with using a tutor is one of authenticity: some students allow the tutor to do too much of the work, and some tutors willingly comply. In such cases, not only is the student deprived of a real learning experience, but the classroom teacher may well notice a difference between the student's usual work and the tutor-aided document.

6. Do your homework with a friend. This is just a great way to turn homework time into fun time. You can satisfy some of your social needs and all of your academic ones. It's a win-win situation . . . as long as you go about it the right way. It's more than OK to talk about the questions and the answers. Just make sure that, when you put pen to paper, your words are not identical. If they are, your teacher will conclude that one of you copied, and it will be impossible for you to prove her wrong.

Let's assume that you've tried the six steps listed above and you still couldn't complete all or part of a homework assignment. Don't despair; it happens to everybody from time to time. You can deal with it the next day.

That next day, do your best to get to school early. That will give you the chance to find someone—a classmate or a teacher—who can help you. If it's just a question of getting a handout, maybe you can manage to complete it during homeroom, lunch, or study hall. If there's something you don't understand, maybe someone can explain it to you.

You may feel you need to discuss this matter with the teacher. In that case, try to get to the teacher before class. Politely explain to the teacher the circumstances that kept you from completing the assignment, and let the teacher know that you are eager to complete the assigned work. Most teachers will be sympathetic, helpful, and flexible. They are much less likely to be sympathetic, helpful, and flexible, however, if you simply fail to produce the work without offering any explanation. Be responsible. Be conscientious.

Once you have gotten the materials and/or assistance you require, make sure you complete the work in a timely manner.

BRAIN TICKLER
Set #11

Life would be a lot easier if every teacher had the same homework policy . . . but they don't. In the very beginning of the year, most teachers take some class time to articulate clearly their homework policies. You and/or your parents may have been asked to sign these.

Have you learned the respective homework policies? If not, are they readily available? Let's see how many of these questions you can answer.

1. How does homework factor into your grade for each course?
2. Does each teacher collect or grade every assignment?
3. How does each teacher grade homework (i.e., letter grades, numerical grades, check/check-plus or –minus)?
4. What is each teacher's policy toward missing homework?
5. What is each teacher's policy toward makeups?

BRAIN TICKLERS
THE ANSWERS

Set #6, page 24

According to the ten-minute rule, a student receives ten minutes of homework for every grade. In other words, a fourth grader would receive forty minutes of homework, an eighth grader twice that.

Answers will vary.

Set #7, page 25

Answers will vary according to the source and the nation. For example, a 2006 report from the Institute of Education Sciences at the U.S. Department of Education reveals that American eighth graders actually spend more time on math homework than do their counterparts in other countries.

Set #8, page 27

Answers will vary.

Set #9, page 34

Answers will vary.

Set # 10, page 37

Here is a model answer to the Nat Turner question.

Nat Turner was an African-American preacher who led a slave revolt in the state of Virginia in 1831. He and his followers ended up killing as many as fifty-seven whites. This led white Virginians to a huge manhunt. Before Turner was found and hanged, many innocent African-Americans were killed. There were several reasons for the small number of slave revolts in the pre-Civil War South. Southern whites were careful about the possibility of slave revolts, and they were much better armed than African-American slaves. Any slave who revolted had to know that he was embarking on some kind of suicide mission since eventually he was sure to be captured and killed.

Set #11, page 41

The important thing is you should know. If you don't, seek clarification from your teachers, or ask for another copy of the policy.

CHAPTER THREE

How to Read a Book
(and You Thought You Knew!)

It all started when you were very little and your parents read poems and stories to you. From there, it was a small step to "reading" your own books. (Even if you couldn't actually read, you probably memorized enough to fill in the blanks or recite the entire book on your own.) Some of these early books may have been of the scratch-and-sniff variety; others may have been textured with soft, furry, or scratchy surfaces. Regardless, you were well on your way. Those pre-school days were hundreds of books ago. Consequently, when it comes to books, you may consider yourself an expert.

Or not.

Different kinds of books require different strategies. The approach you bring to reading, say, twenty pages of a novel is different from the one you bring to answering three comprehension questions at the end of a chapter in your science text.

Keep this in mind as you work your way through this chapter.

GETTING TO KNOW YOUR TEXTBOOK

Textbooks have become extremely expensive, and they tend to weigh a ton, but schools continue to use them because they contain a great deal of information. Your typical textbook will cover a year's worth of material. And you will be using textbooks of increasing size and complexity throughout your educational career.

So it's important to get to know the one you have in your hand.

Begin by examining the table of contents. The table of contents lists the chapters in the book and therefore tells you how the book is organized. An American history textbook would be organized chronologically, beginning with the exploration and colonization of America and ending with relatively current events. In addition, while some tables of contents are more detailed than others, each offers some information about the makeup of each chapter. As you scan a table of contents, you will see how each chapter is organized. The organization of most textbooks tends to be consistent from chapter to chapter. Consequently, you will know what to expect as you work your way through the book.

BRAIN TICKLER
Set #12

Examine this sample entry from a table of contents of a book about grammar and writing. Then answer the questions that follow.

Chapter 7: Writing Really Good Sentences 376

1. How are font sizes used to help the reader understand how the chapter is organized?

2. Where would you turn for a good definition of a complex sentence?

3. Where would you look if your teacher told you that some of your sentences tend to run on?

4. What do you think is the purpose of the section entitled "Putting It All Together"?

After you have finished looking at the table of contents, turn to the other end of the book. There you will find the index. Once you become familiar with your textbook, you will probably have more occasions to use the index than you will the table of contents. Because the index is arranged in alphabetical order, you can immediately find whatever topic you're looking for.

Let's say you're reading a chapter in your social studies text, and you come across the expression "judicial review." It sounds familiar, but you don't know exactly what it means or when you first encountered it. Your first move? Turn to the index. There you might find an entry that looks like this:

judicial review
  in U.S. Constitution 189
  Marbury v. Madison 207

As soon as you see "*Marbury* v. *Madison*," you say to yourself, "That's where I heard it! The Supreme Court case!" You turn to page 207, read the material, and recall that the principle of judicial review gives the Supreme Court the power to declare laws unconstitutional.

BRAIN TICKLER
Set #13

Examine this index entry from a typical math text. Then answer the two questions that follow.

cylinder
  area of 435
  base of 434
  comparison to other geometric
    solids 437
  definition 433
  volume of 435

1. Where would you turn to find the formula needed to determine the volume of a cylinder?

2. Where would you turn to learn how a cylinder is similar to or different from a cube?

Now that you have checked out the table of contents and the index, it's time to turn to the glossary. A glossary is a mini-dictionary of terms specific to a particular text. Not every textbook has one, of course, but most do. If you look in the glossary of your American history text, you will probably find an entry corresponding to "judicial review." The definition provided there will not supply as much information as you would obtain by using the index and the referenced pages within, but it is certainly faster.

A foreign language textbook has a highly specialized glossary. In fact, it may well have two glossaries. The first will translate from the foreign language to English, and the second will provide the foreign language equivalent of English words. Both are very useful.

BRAIN TICKLER
Set #14

1. Use the glossary of your science textbook to obtain a good definition of *hypothesis*.

2. Use the glossary of your social studies textbook to obtain a good definition of *hieroglyphics*.

3. Use the glossary of your math textbook to obtain a good definition of *hypotenuse*.

4. Use the glossary of your foreign language textbook to obtain a good definition of *hypocrite*.

Glossaries and indexes are fairly standard features of textbooks. As you scour your textbooks, you will learn that they possess as many as two hundred pages of other, specialized features. Take a basic American history text, for example. You may very well discover these features:

- A copy of the Declaration of Independence
- A copy of the Constitution of the United States
- A list of famous speeches
- A geographic atlas

- A list of historical sites (sometimes known as a gazetteer)
- Biographical information about the Presidents of the United States
- Information pertaining to American literature, art, music, and science

Look at yours. Did you find anything else? Any additional surprises?

BRAIN TICKLER
Set #15

Locate your science textbook. Your book certainly contains a table of contents, index, and glossary. What other special sections can you locate?

HOW TO READ A CHAPTER IN A GENERAL TEXTBOOK

Before you actually delve into your required chapter readings, you need to preview the chapter. In most textbooks, chapters are organized similarly, each with similar or identical features. Some textbooks actually contain brief introductory sections explaining how the chapters are organized.

Here are some steps you can take to gain a solid overall sense of a chapter in a textbook:

1. Read the chapter title.

2. Read the introductory paragraph. (Many chapters will offer a paragraph that explains in a general way the contents of that chapter.)

3. Read the subchapter headings. The textbook will employ different fonts or boldface so that you can easily identify these.

4. Look quickly at the charts, pictures, graphs, tables, cartoons, and the like. Read the captions under each.

5. Read the concluding paragraph or summary.

6. Read the questions at the end of the chapter.

All of these steps will take you just a few minutes. This is time well spent.

So let's assume you have fully familiarized yourself with the text and the chapter. Now it's time to do the assignment. Read the assignment carefully; if the assignment requires you to answer questions from the text, take a quick look at those.

Now you are faced with a couple of important questions.

Your first question is simply this: do you have to read *everything*, or do you just need to read enough of the assigned pages to answer the questions satisfactorily? Let's face it: it's easy enough to read the questions first, then use key words from the questions to locate pertinent passages in the text.

To read or not to read. That is the question.

Let's say you come across this question in your history textbook: "Why did President Andrew Jackson oppose the Bank of the United States?" You scan the chapter until you find a subheading, "The Bank War," and in that section a paragraph heading, "Jackson vetoes the bill." You've hit paydirt.

Now there's nothing wrong with your taking that approach. You can employ that strategy and still do an excellent job on your homework. But before you decide to take that shortcut, you need to keep in mind these concerns:

• To what extent are you responsible for all the material in the reading? Will your teacher give you a quiz the following day to make sure you've read it all? Will your teacher go over all the material the following day, or will you be expected to learn and retain it on your own?

- How does your short-range goal of saving time stack up against your long-range goal of becoming a better student? In other words, are you interested merely in submitting acceptable homework, or are you genuinely interested in learning the material? Will the information about Jackson's veto mean as much to you if you haven't acquired a fuller picture of his presidency? Are you content with acquiring the necessary information in class when the teacher reviews the material, or do you wish to become a leader in the next day's discussion?

These are decisions that you have to make, as you consider time, motivation, and interest.

Question #2: should you take notes as you read? (Later in this book, you will read about taking notes and creating outlines. These are two invaluable skills for serious students.) Here's the rule of thumb: if you're going to have to take notes eventually, you may as well do it now. At some point, your teacher is going to test you on certain material, and you will need to study your notes. What will those notes include? Will you be studying outlines or study guides completed in class? Will your teacher suggest that you review your homework answers? Will you be asked to study the quizzes leading up to that test?

Or . . . will your teacher simply tell you that you are responsible for the material in a particular chapter? If that's the case, then you should take good notes when you first encounter the material. This way, you will be well-prepared for class, and you will save a great deal of time later on.

Major Mistake Territory!

If you know that your teacher will require you to study from chapter notes, it would be a serious error on your part to leave note-taking (and outline-creating) for the night or two before the test. It's simply too much work; it's way too time-consuming, especially if you're dealing with several chapters. Not only that: you want to avoid duplication of effort. After all, you've already read the material when you did your homework; why force yourself to read it a second time if you don't have to?

HOW TO READ A FOREIGN LANGUAGE TEXTBOOK

When you are reading a foreign language textbook, keep in mind this formula:

P3R.

The "P" stands for **Preview**:

- Scan the chapter to be read.
- Check for new vocabulary.
- Check for new grammatical structures.
- Check for new information pertaining to culture.

The first "R" stands for **Relate**:

- When possible, relate new vocabulary to previously learned words.
- Be aware of similarities in grammar and construction between English and the language you are studying.

The second "R" stands for **Read**:

- Read each sentence from the beginning to the end without looking up words.
- Try to guess the meaning of new words.
- Look up words to verify your guesses only after you have read each sentence and cannot make sense of the meaning. (Keep handy a good foreign language dictionary.)
- Read aloud. This gives you additional oral practice.
- Read the selections until you know them.
- Reread.

The final "R" stands for **Review**:

- Learn the required vocabulary.
- Memorize grammatical structures and verbs given in each chapter.
- Work with another student to review.
- Drill as often as necessary.

P3R: that's a formula worth remembering. In fact, you will see it again—very soon.

HOW TO READ A MATH TEXTBOOK

Once again the formula P3R comes into play.

P = Preview! Look over the chapter to find

- the process you will use to solve problems;
- the kinds of problems you will learn to solve; and
- whether the chapter is based on previous lessons or totally new material.

R = Relate! Remember that

- in math, everything new is related in some way to a previously learned skill or concept.
- you should always try to relate math problems or examples to something in your own personal experience.

R = Read!

- Read all instructions and explanations carefully.
- Reread as often as you need.
- Learn the rules in the chapter.
- Apply the rules by solving the sample problem.
- Read word problems carefully so that you know precisely what is being asked of you.

R = Review!

- Go over your classwork daily. You will notice the connection between classwork and textbook material.
- Memorize. Go over material you must know instantly in order to solve math problems.
- Make reference lists of such things as vocabulary, important rules, and frequently used formulas.

Now let's see whether you can apply these strategies.

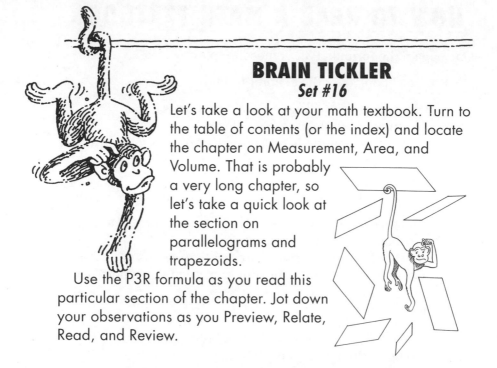

BRAIN TICKLER
Set #16

Let's take a look at your math textbook. Turn to the table of contents (or the index) and locate the chapter on Measurement, Area, and Volume. That is probably a very long chapter, so let's take a quick look at the section on parallelograms and trapezoids.

Use the P3R formula as you read this particular section of the chapter. Jot down your observations as you Preview, Relate, Read, and Review.

HOW TO READ LITERATURE

There may have been a time when to many the term *literature* was practically synonymous with *fiction*, but that time has passed. These days, readers assign a broader definition to that term. *Literature* encompasses not only the many categories of fiction (such as short stories, novels, poems, and plays) but those of nonfiction (such as essays, articles, biographies, autobiographies, and histories) as well.

Even though all these different genres of literature differ from each other in significant ways, they also share some of the same characteristics. Consequently, they require of the reader certain common skills.

As you read any work of literature, you need to be mindful of these five elements: character, plot, setting, narration, and theme.

Understanding Character

A character is a person or animal who takes part in the action of a literary work. Some characters are major, others minor.

We learn about character in four ways:

- The author directly tells us about the character. ("Jersey Simmons was a sweet-tempered, generous soul.")
- The character tells us about him- or herself. ("For as long as I can remember, I always wanted to treat people kindly.")
- Other characters tell us about the character. ("Martin Simmons said, 'I can't imagine being married to a woman more attentive or affectionate than Jersey.'")
- The character's actions and words tell us about him or her. ("Whenever Jersey Simmons came home from work, she made sure to greet her husband and children warmly.")

Be alert to the following when thinking about character development:

- Physical appearance. What does the character look like? What is the connection between physical appearance and other personality traits?
- Personality. What are the characteristics that make up the character's personality? Is she generous or selfish? Is she cynical or naïve? Is she lazy or ambitious? Is she cruel or kind? What are the character's strengths and weaknesses?
- Character dimensions. A "round" character is fully developed: realistically portrayed, multifaceted, unpredictable. A "flat" character is predictable, stereotypical, one-dimensional.

BRAIN TICKLER
Set #17

Read the following passage from Charles Dickens's novel, *Great Expectations*. What do you learn about two characters, Joe Gargery and his wife, Mrs. Joe Gargery? How do you acquire this information? (Note: this passage is narrated by Pip, an orphan who is raised by his sister, Mrs. Joe, and Joe.)

My sister, Mrs. Joe Gargery, was more than twenty years older than I, and had established a great reputation with herself and the neighbors because she had brought me up "by hand." Having at that time to find out myself what the expression meant, and knowing her to have a hard and heavy hand, and to be much in the habit of laying it upon her husband as well as upon me, I supposed that Joe Gargery and I were both brought up by hand.

She was not a good-looking woman, my sister, and I had a general impression that she must have made Joe Gargery marry her by hand. Joe was a fair man, with curls and flaxen hair on each side of his smooth face, and with eyes of such a very undecided blue that they seemed to have somehow got mixed with their own whites. He was a mild, good-natured, sweet-tempered, easy-going, foolish dear fellow—a sort of Hercules in strength, and also in weakness.

Understanding Plot

The plot is the sequence of events that keeps the story moving toward its conclusion. When a friend asks you about a movie, you are most likely to tell him what happens in the movie. That's the plot.

In some works of literature, plot plays a central role. If you think about an action movie or a spy novel, you are thinking about an event that is most likely plot-driven. In other works, plot may play a relatively minor role, and another element, usually character, dominates.

These are the main ingredients of the plot:

- The **conflict** drives the plot. A good reader should be able to identify the conflicts. An **internal conflict** is a struggle that a character has with himself: for example, should I study for my Spanish exam, or should I watch Monday Night Football? An **external conflict** is a struggle that a character has with either another character, a force of nature, or the state.

- The **climax** (or **crisis**) is the high point of interest or suspense, usually because the main character acts in order to resolve his or her conflicts. For example, you may decide that since Spanish comes first, you will TiVo the football game and watch it later. The climax is the turning point of the story.
- The **resolution** is the outcome or result of the climax.

BRAIN TICKLER
Set #18

Read this first paragraph from the famous short story, "The Necklace," by Guy de Maupassant. See if you can identify the conflict. What kind of conflict is it?

> She was one of those pretty and charming girls born, as though fate had blundered over her, into a family of artisans. She had no marriage portion, no expectations, no means of getting known, understood, loved, and wedded by a man of wealth and distinction; and she let herself be married off to a little clerk in the Ministry of Education. Her tastes were simple because she had never been able to afford any other, but she was as unhappy as though she had married beneath her; for women have no caste or class, their beauty, grace, and charm serving them for birth or family, their natural delicacy, their instinctive elegance, their nimbleness of wit, are their only mark of rank, and put the slum girl on a level with the highest lady in the land.

Understanding Setting

The setting is the time and place in which an author places his or her story. Is the story set in the past, present, or future? Is it set in a particular place? Above all, what difference does the setting make?

Admittedly, sometimes the author's choice of setting has little or no impact on the reader's understanding and appreciation of the story, but that's a relatively rare occurrence.

If you were reading a biography of Abraham Lincoln, you could not possibly fail to consider the turbulent times in which Lincoln lived: a country torn by political, economic, and social issues. As President, Lincoln faced three enormous challenges. He needed to win a war, unify a nation, and grant freedom to a large group of Americans.

Take, for example, a work of nonfiction called *The Boys of Summer*, written by Roger Kahn. Kahn's book was published in 1971, but concerns itself with the Brooklyn Dodgers baseball team of the early 1950s. Why is that information important? Well, for one thing, Kahn writes about an era in which baseball was king. Football and basketball were little more than wispy clouds on the faraway sports horizon. Soccer? Maybe a few people could tell you it was a game played by residents of Europe or South America. The point is this: Americans were just nuts about baseball and followed it with an intensity that today's fans probably cannot imagine. They listened to games on transistor radios and avidly read articles in the next day's newspaper. They debated vigorously whether one team or one player was better than another.

Second, Jackie Robinson was a player on that Dodger team. Today the presence of African-Americans on any major sports team is no surprise, but in 1947 Robinson broke the color barrier in baseball. In Kahn's book, the reactions of Robinson's teammates and opponents, as well as those of the fans, play an important part.

BRAIN TICKLER
Set #19

Go to your library (or go online) to get some information about a novel called *Farewell to Manzanar* by Jeanne Wakatsuki Houston. Why does setting play an important part in this novel?

Understanding Narration

A narrator is the person who tells a story. The way the story is told is called narration, or point of view. An author's choice of narrator and point of view determines the kind of information the reader will be given. It may also reflect a particular bias.

The most commonly used points of view are

- First person. The narrator ("I," "me") is a character in the story. A first person narrator can reveal only his own thoughts and feelings and what he is told by other characters.

  EXAMPLE:
  Jamie and I had been friends for a long time. I couldn't understand why she suddenly stopped calling me.

- Third person limited omniscient. The narrator, not a character in the story, observes events mainly from the perspective of one character.

  EXAMPLE:
  Because they had been friends for a long time, Pete couldn't understand why Jamie had stopped calling him.

- Third person omniscient. The narrator, not a character in the story, is an all-knowing outsider who can enter the minds of one or all of the characters.

EXAMPLE:
Because they had been friends for a long time, Pete couldn't understand why Jamie had stopped calling him. What Pete didn't realize was that Jamie had long wanted out of the friendship.

In the short story, "The Necklace," the author chooses a third person limited omniscient narrator. The narrator is not a character in the story; events are told from the perspective of the main character, Mathilde Loisel. When Mathilde borrows a "diamond" necklace from her wealthy friend, she doesn't know that the diamonds are phony. Later, she loses the necklace, replaces it with a real one, and spends ten years paying off her debts. Only at the very end of the story—the very last line, in fact—does Mathilde learn that the necklace is "false." The author's decision to use this point of view keeps this fact from Mathilde and ensures the effectiveness of the story's ironic ending.

As you are reading, not only must you be aware of how the story is related and by whom, but you also must consider the narrator's bias. When you read an opinion piece, such as an editorial in a newspaper, the writer's bias may be plain to see. In a work of fiction, however, a narrator's bias may be harder to detect.

Jane Austen's wonderful novel, *Pride and Prejudice*, begins this way:

> *It is a truth universally acknowledged that a single man in possession of a good fortune must be in want of a wife.*
> *However little known the feelings or views of such a man may be on his first entering a neighbourhood, this truth is so well fixed in the minds of the surrounding families that he is considered as the rightful property of some one or other of their daughters.*

What can you conclude about this narrator? Well, for one thing, you can tell that she is not a character in the story. You can also conclude that she is very clever . . . and not a little cynical, either. Her point is that the residents of a particular neighborhood, pleased to hear of the arrival of a single, wealthy male newcomer, will think of such a man as destined for one of their daughters—and it doesn't really matter what *he* thinks about the matter.

BRAIN TICKLER
Set #20
Read this beginning of Robert Louis Stevenson's novel, *Treasure Island*. What do you learn of its narration?

Squire Trelawny, Dr. Livesey, and the rest of these gentlemen having asked me to write down the whole particulars about Treasure Island, from the beginning to the end, keeping nothing back but the bearings of the island, and that only because there is still treasure not yet lifted, I take up my pen in the year of grace 17— and go back to the time when my father kept the Admiral Benbow inn and the brown and old seaman with the sabre cut first took up his lodging under our roof.

Understanding Theme

A theme is a central message of a literary work. It is an important idea that the author wishes to convey to the reader.

Students sometimes have a hard time figuring out the theme of a work. Here are three strategies you can adopt to help you determine the theme:

1. Think about the main character's conflict and the story's climax. If, at the story's climax, the main character acts decisively in order to resolve the conflict, what can you, the reader, conclude about this action? Why did the character take that action?

2. State the theme as a sentence. For example, it is not sufficient to say that the theme of the story is "independence"; it is better to say that the theme is that children at some point must learn to make up their own minds. Remember: the theme is the *point* of the story; it is not the *topic*.

3. How does the title of the work relate to the theme?

Major Mistake Territory!

Don't confuse theme with plot. Which of these is a proper statement of theme?

- A young man, faced with the challenge of swimming through an underwater tunnel, exercises discipline and rigorous training in order to succeed at the task.
- Exercising discipline and will in the completion of a formidable task can be an important step in growing up.

The first describes what happens in Doris Lessing's short story, "Through the Tunnel." Therefore, it is a statement of the story's plot. The second is a statement of the story's main point. As such, it is a good statement of theme.

BRAIN TICKLER
Set #21

Read this poem by A. E. Housman. Then decide which of the statements below is the best statement of the poem's theme.

Loveliest of Trees

Loveliest of trees, the cherry now
Is hung with bloom along the bough,
And stand about the woodland ride*
Wearing white for Eastertide.

*a road for riding

Now, of my threescore years and ten*
Twenty will not come again,
And take from seventy springs a score,
It only leaves me fifty more.

*seventy years (an average life span)

And since to look at things in bloom
Fifty springs are little room,
About the woodlands I will go
To see the cherry hung with snow.

a. Sometimes nature can be a real annoyance.

b. We don't live forever, so it's important to enjoy life's special pleasures.

c. A seemingly random or insignificant event can change one's mood or outlook.

How to Read a Play

In contemporary life, we are accustomed to seeing plays, whether we view movies and TV shows or occasionally enjoy the opportunity to see a play performed on stage. For most of us, reading a play is something that will happen only in English or drama classes. The next time you have that chance, consider these suggestions:

Preview the material:

- For starters, read the title.
- Look inside for any pertinent introductory material. A Shakespearean play, for example, would probably include some background material on the subject of the play, on Shakespeare's life, and on theatrical conventions of that time.
- Take a look at the cast of characters. (Sometimes this is called the *dramatis personae*.) Typically, this will list the characters in order of importance and will identify each. Don't hesitate to turn back to this section as you read.

- Read the description of the setting. Prior to each act (or scene), a playwright generally offers a description of what the audience will see.

As you read:

- Visualize! Try to see the scenes in your mind as if you were viewing them on the stage.
- Read the stage directions carefully so that you can appreciate the characters' movements and emotions.

Reflect:

- Stop at the end of each scene to think about what you have read. Summarize the events that have unfolded.
- Think about unresolved conflicts. Think about the connection between character and actions.
- Make predictions about what will happen in ensuing scenes.

How to Read a Poem

Why are poems so hard to understand?

First of all, not all of them are. Here's one that's kind of easy:

> *I suppose that plumbers' children know more about plumbing than plumbers do, and welders' children know more about welding than welders,*
> *Because the only fact in an implausible world is that all young know better than their elders.*

from "There's Nothing Like Instinct, Fortunately," by Ogden Nash

Why is this poem easy? For one thing, it doesn't sound like poetry. "Welders" rhymes with "elders," but that's about all. It reads like prose (that is, sentences and paragraphs), even if it looks like lines of poetry. Second, it doesn't contain any difficult language (only *implausible*, which means "unlikely," is a challenging word), and it doesn't contain the kind of dense language we associate with poetry.

Of course, not all poems you come across will present themselves as clearly as the one above. In that case, here are some strategies that will help:

1. Read the title of the poem. Think about what the title might mean. Sometimes the title will help you understand a poem that would otherwise be difficult. Sometimes the title can provide an important clue to the poem's meaning.

2. Read the poem aloud. Read the poem slowly. You will need to read the poem more than once.

3. As you read the poem, be careful about pauses. Sometimes poems are written as a collection of sentences; if not, they almost always consist of complete units of thought. Don't pause just because you've reached the end of the line.

Major Mistake Territory!

Consider the first stanza of A. E. Housman's "Loveliest of Trees":

> Loveliest of trees, the cherry now
> Is hung with bloom along the bough,
> And stands about the woodland ride
> Wearing white for Eastertide.

You will notice that this first stanza actually consists of one sentence. You will also notice that only lines 2 and 4 end with punctuation that tells the reader to pause. If you pause at the end of every line, the poem becomes harder to understand. Learn to read this way, pausing only when the poet's punctuation tells you to do so.

4. Words are important. Have a dictionary nearby so that you can look up unfamiliar words.

5. Pay careful attention to imagery and figurative language. Poets use words to create sensory pictures; this we call **imagery**. Poets also employ creative comparisons; these we call **figurative language** (sometimes *figures of speech*). You are no doubt familiar with metaphors, similes, and

personification. Examine the use of personification, for example, in the Housman poem above. Cherry trees do not really "wear white"; only people dress up for Eastertide.

6. Above all, look for meaning in the poem. Reread the stanzas and try to put them in your own words. Try to explain the poet's feelings about the subject of the poem. Think about how the poem makes you feel.

BRAIN TICKLER
Set #22

Read the poem "Travel," by Edna St. Vincent Millay. Try out your poetry reading skills by answering the questions that follow.

> The railroad track is miles away,
> And the day is loud with speaking;
> Yet there isn't a train goes by all day
> But I hear its whistle shrieking.
>
> All night there isn't a train goes by,
> Though the night is still for sleep and dreaming,
> But I see its cinders red on the sky,
> And I hear its engine steaming.
>
> My heart is warm with the friends I make,
> And better friends I'll not be knowing,
> Yet there isn't a train I wouldn't take,
> No matter where it's going.

1. What images dominate the poem?
2. What is the poem's central idea? How do you know?

WHEN READING IS TOUGH

Sometimes you might have to deal with a particularly difficult reading assignment. If you are just not getting it, try some of the following techniques:

- Do it while you're fresh. Don't save difficult reading for late in the evening when you're tired and you can't concentrate so well. It might be a good idea to make this your very first homework task while you're at your very best.
- Read it again. Difficult reading material, such as technical passages or primary sources, may require a second reading. If you're not getting it, if you've stopped concentrating, go back and read it again. Budget your time accordingly.
- Break it down. Read small sections. Stop at the end of each section and recite, in your own words, what you have read.
- Read it aloud. Imagine you are the author talking.
- Get an audiotape or CD. Of course, this is not always an option, but it often is with novels and plays.

As you further your education and as you enter the world of work, you will often have to deal with challenging reading material. Some of this material may interest you, but some may simply be a class or job requirement. It's important that you develop the discipline and strategies to meet this challenge. Now is a great time to start.

BRAIN TICKLERS
THE ANSWERS

Set #12, page 48

1. Each chapter is divided into sections and subsections. The largest font is used to identify the chapter's title. The next largest identifies the sections of the chapter, and the smallest is used to designate the subsections.
2. Turn to page 387.
3. Fix your run-ons on page 379.
4. The last section, "Putting It All Together," is probably a review activity for the entire chapter.

Set #13, page 49

1. page 435
2. page 437

Set #14, page 50

1. hypothesis—a proposed solution to a scientific problem
2. hieroglyphics—a system of writing that uses pictures to represent words and ideas
3. hypotenuse—the side of a right triangle that is opposite the right angle
4. hypocrite—answers will vary; however, the Spanish equivalent of *hypocrite* is *hypócrita*. The French equivalent is *hypocrite*.

Set #15, page 51

Answers will vary, according to the text.

A typical physical science textbook might contain information pertaining to commonly used metric units, safety rules, mathematical processes, and science formulas. In addition, you could surely expect to find a periodic table of the elements, as well as other information about the elements.

Set #16, page 56

Answers will vary, according to the text and your individual reaction to it. However, your observations might resemble these:

Preview

- This chapter is mostly about figuring out the areas of parallelograms and trapezoids.
- It is based on what I already know about triangles and rectangles.

Relate

- Lots of the terminology seems familiar (base, height), and I already know how to do the computations.
- I can see how this material would be helpful to solve word problems or for designing or building things.

Read

- The important rules in the chapter have to do with the two key formulas.
- I was able to solve the sample problems.

Review

- The two formulas I need to know are the area of a parallelogram ($A = b \times h$) and a trapezoid ($A = \frac{1}{2} (b_1 + b_2)h$).

Set #17, page 57

Answers will vary.

The reader learns that Mrs. Joe Gargery is not attractive physically or personally. Pip, the narrator, says the former directly. The reader may infer that Mrs. Joe is somewhat abusive because she has applied her "hard and heavy hand" to Joe and Pip.

The reader learns that Joe is in many ways the opposite of Mrs. Joe. The narrator says that he is "fair" and later goes on to list a number of positive character traits ("mild, good-natured" and so on). Pip also says that Mrs. Joe "must have made Joe Gargery marry her by hand"; in other words, he cannot understand how Joe would agree to marry her unless he were forced to do so. His final statement, that Joe is "a sort of Hercules in strength, and also in weakness," alludes to the fact that Joe may have been physically powerful, but intellectually limited.

Set #18, page 59

This is a difficult passage because it presents contradictory information. The "she" of the paragraph, Mathilde Loisel, is a very pretty, graceful, witty girl, and as such belongs to no class: she is "on a level with the highest lady in the land." However, despite her personal attractiveness, she very clearly belongs to a particular social class. It is lower than the one she would like to belong to, and she feels stuck in it. Therefore, you could say her conflict is internal because she desires to be wealthier than she is. On the other hand, you could say her conflict is external because she lives in a world that does not permit movement from a lower class to a higher one.

Set #19, page 61

Farewell to Manzanar is set in California in 1941, right after Japanese planes bombed Pearl Harbor. The novel's main characters are Japanese-American citizens, who, as a result of this unfortunate event, were then subjected to a great deal of anti-Japanese sentiment. At one point, they are confined to internment camps.

Set #20, page 63

The novel is narrated from a first person point of view. It seems as if the narrator has returned from an adventure and has been asked by some "gentleman" to relate their shared story. Probably the narrator is a bit younger than these gentlemen, and, since his father is an innkeeper, he is probably of a lower class.

Set #21, page 64

The correct answer is "b." Statement "a" is altogether inaccurate. Statement "b" goes beyond the immediate events of the poem to capture the narrator's point and is therefore the best statement of theme. Statement "c" refers to "random events," but there is nothing random about the narrator's appreciation of the cherry blossoms.

Set #22, page 68

1. Answers will vary but might include "hear its whistle shrieking," "see its cinders red on the sky," and "hear its engine steaming."

2. The poem's central idea is the narrator's desire to travel. First of all, the title offers a clue. Second is the fact that, day or night, every passing train captures the narrator's attention. Finally, in the last stanza, the narrator says that, regardless of the fine friends she already has, she wouldn't pass on the chance to jump on any train, "No matter where it's going."

CHAPTER FOUR

Taking Notes: Capturing the Content

It's one thing to work very hard on getting ready for tests and projects, and much of this book will help you do just that. However, you need to understand that certain skills are so fundamental that without them academic success is highly unlikely. In other words, before you can get serious about studying for tests and preparing for projects, you have to develop skills that will enable you to study effectively.

Of these skills, none is more important than learning to take good notes. And even though the thought of taking notes may elicit a ho-hum yawn and a "been-there-done-that," you should not be misled: learning to take good notes is a powerful step in taking control of your own lifelong education.

BRAIN TICKLER
Set #23

Note-taking is essential to academic situations: whether you are in middle school, high school, college, or beyond, you will need to take good notes in order to succeed. However, note-taking is just as essential to *non academic* situations. Can you think of five non-academic situations in which you would need to take notes?

When you were younger, your teachers *gave* you all the notes you would need. Perhaps your teacher wrote notes on the board and asked the class to copy them. Or maybe you were given a handout containing in note form the material you were expected to learn. In any case, at some point you were expected to take a more active role. Your teachers insisted that you look, listen, and think.

We use the expression *to take note of* as a synonym of *to notice*. No matter where you are seated in the ballpark, you are sure to notice the distinctive crack that results from Barry Bonds's bat crushing an imperfectly thrown fastball. However, you will only notice the hot dog vendor if your growling stomach is telling you it must be fed—and soon. In other words, some phenomena grab our attention, but much of our attention is selective. And that's where discipline comes in. When you're riding your bike, you would *prefer* to listen raptly to the tunes on your MP3 player, but you know you *must* focus on vehicular and pedestrian traffic.

Most academic situations require you to attend to a combination of auditory (that is, spoken) and visual (printed) material. If you think about a typical math or social studies class, you will realize that sometimes you are expected to listen to what is being said by your teacher, your classmates, or some other speaker, and sometimes on your own you must examine words, images, numerals, and symbols. But it would be very unusual for you to spend an entire forty-minute period doing only one of these two kinds of activities.

Nevertheless, this chapter will consider the two skills separately.

LEARNING TO LISTEN

There is a very big difference between hearing and listening. Hearing is one of your five senses, but listening is a skill that uses that sense. Your ability to hear may be perfect, but that doesn't mean you are a good listener.

Are you the kind of person people come to with their problems? If so, that could be the result of two related reasons. The first is simply that you are a good listener. Most of the time, people just need a friendly ear, someone who will listen to their concerns without selfishly interrupting or judging. A second reason could be that, having listened carefully, you are the kind of person who asks good questions and gives sound advice.

BRAIN TICKLER
Set #24

Evaluate yourself as a listener. Are you the kind of person people come to with their problems? How would your parents evaluate you as a listener? How would your friends evaluate you?

Think about one friend whom you would describe as a good listener. What does that person actually do that makes him or her such a good listener?

Listening well is to some extent a matter of discipline. Let's face it: you are not automatically interested in listening to your social studies teacher discuss the causes of the War of 1812. While your math teacher explains how to solve linear equations, you just might be more interested in the lacrosse game you have later that afternoon. And when your best friend goes on and on about her annoying younger brother, you might be tempted to tell her that she's complained about him every day for the last three years and you're tired of hearing it.

But you exercise discipline. You set aside your own needs and preferences in order to focus on what someone else is saying.

When you evaluated your friend's listening abilities, you listed a set of behaviors you associated with good listening. If listening is a matter of behaving in a particular way, then those behaviors can be duplicated in order to improve your own listening abilities.

Here are some listening skills that you can actually practice:

1. Stay in the room! Teachers don't like to get into arguments with students about hall passes; as a result, many have devised sign-out books so that students can leave the room without disrupting the class. Nevertheless, teachers know that while most students *never* ask to leave the room, a small group of students routinely find reasons to be elsewhere. In which category do you fall? If you're not in the room, you can't listen to what's being said. When you return, it's hard to get back in the flow.

2. Maintain good body language! Sit straight. Face whoever is speaking, and try to keep some eye contact with the speaker.

3. Show the speaker you are attending! You may notice that, when you are speaking to a friend, you will nod your head to let that person know you have been listening to what he or she is saying and that you understand and perhaps agree. Even when you are using the phone, every half-minute or so you will say, "Uh-huh," just to let your friend know you're still there and still paying attention. In a classroom setting, you cannot have thirty students simultaneously muttering, "Uh-huh," but an occasional nod of the head will let the speaker know you're there and on task.

4. Interact with the speaker! It's one thing to hear what a speaker is saying and another to listen. However, the best compliment that you can pay a speaker is to let him or her know that you've been *thinking* about what's been said. As we've said, maintaining good body language and nodding let the speaker know you've been listening. The next step involves your speaking with the speaker. Here are some ways you can do that:

   A. You want to listen, but a soft speaker is straining your auditory capabilities. Raise your hand and let the speaker know that he or she is speaking too softly. After all, in so doing, aren't you letting the speaker know that his or her words are important to you?

B. Ask the speaker to explain what he or she has said. You know that sometimes words can simply get in the way of clarity. Sometimes we think we're saying something, but people are hearing something else. Sometimes it can be enough simply to say, "Can you give an example?" Asking a speaker to clarify his or her thoughts can be very helpful to both the speaker and his or her audience.

C. Challenge the speaker. If you accept without questioning whatever a speaker says, you are not holding that person to a very high standard. You are giving him or her the message that, intellectually, anything goes and that you really don't care to invest a great deal of energy in whatever he or she happens to be saying. On the other hand, when you politely challenge a speaker, you are paying him or her a compliment. You are demonstrating that you've paid attention and that you've seriously considered what has been said. Having done so, you are well within your rights to ask the speaker to support his or her facts or to explain his or her reasoning.

Major Mistake Territory!

You will notice that the word *politely* appears in the preceding paragraph. Remember that when you challenge a speaker, you are not throwing down the gauntlet and asking him or her to choose weapons. You are tactfully and respectfully questioning or disagreeing. You are trying your very hardest not to show up someone else. When you and your classmates get serious about listening, your classroom becomes an open marketplace of ideas. That can be an exciting development, but it also contains an element of danger. By exercising good manners, you can minimize that danger.

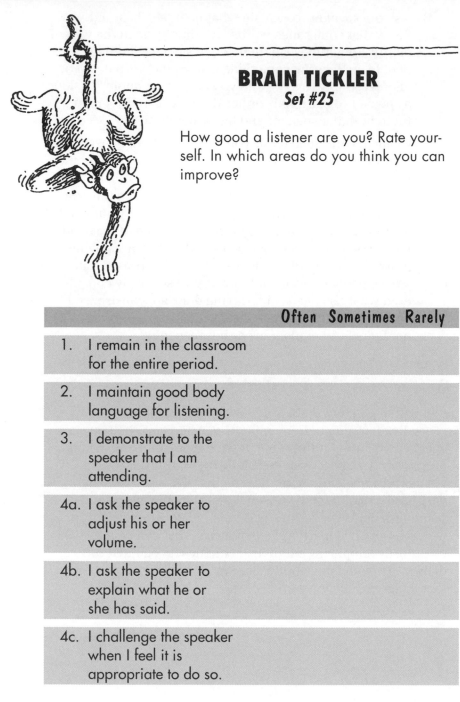

BRAIN TICKLER
Set #25

How good a listener are you? Rate yourself. In which areas do you think you can improve?

		Often	Sometimes	Rarely
1.	I remain in the classroom for the entire period.			
2.	I maintain good body language for listening.			
3.	I demonstrate to the speaker that I am attending.			
4a.	I ask the speaker to adjust his or her volume.			
4b.	I ask the speaker to explain what he or she has said.			
4c.	I challenge the speaker when I feel it is appropriate to do so.			

TAKING NOTES FROM AUDITORY SOURCES

Now that you are well on your way to becoming a listener of the very highest rank, you are prepared to direct your attention to taking notes.

There are no hard-and-fast rules for taking notes when listening, but here are a few helpful guidelines:

1. Give your notes a title, and record the date. That way, days or weeks later, you will quickly be able to determine the subject.

2. Try to record as much information as you can. Generally, the more notes you have taken, the easier it will be to complete the tasks that follow.

3. That said, do *not* attempt to record word for word every utterance you have heard. No matter how quickly you can write, you will inevitably fall behind.

4. Listen for important details and facts. Record these in bullet form.

5. Listen for main ideas. Record these in bullet form.

6. Use symbols ($, &, #, @, ->) and abbreviations (e.g., etc., re) whenever possible. As you become comfortable with note-taking, you will develop your own set of useful symbols. One common kind of abbreviation is acronyms (words created from the first letters of other words—for example, Amex stands for the American Stock Exchange).

7. Develop your own shorthand. For example, if you are listening to a speech about recent developments in television technology, you might substitute "hd" for "high definition" or "pl" for "plasma."

8. Don't worry about words whose meanings you don't know. Sometimes you will be given a vocabulary list. If not, you can always ask afterwards.

9. Sometimes—on certain state tests, for example—you will be given a second reading of a passage. If that is the case, you need to decide on a note-taking strategy. Given the choice, most students decide to take notes during the first reading and during the second fill in whatever they may have missed.

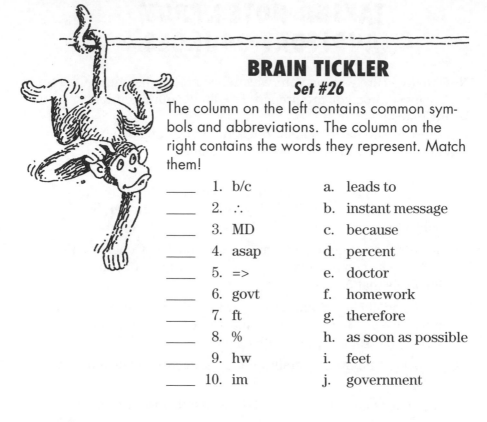

BRAIN TICKLER
Set #26

The column on the left contains common symbols and abbreviations. The column on the right contains the words they represent. Match them!

_____ 1. b/c   a. leads to

_____ 2. ∴   b. instant message

_____ 3. MD   c. because

_____ 4. asap   d. percent

_____ 5. =>   e. doctor

_____ 6. govt   f. homework

_____ 7. ft   g. therefore

_____ 8. %   h. as soon as possible

_____ 9. hw   i. feet

_____ 10. im   j. government

Let's pretend that your teacher has asked each student in the class to speak for a couple of minutes about an interest that he or she has developed. Because your teacher is also concerned with teaching listening and note-taking skills, he has asked students to keep themselves busy by taking notes.

The very first speaker—let's call him "Matt"—is an outgoing young man who is eager to share with the class his particular area of expertise. Here is his speech:

Some of you may not know that FIFA stands for Fédération Internationale de Football Association. When we Americans think of football, we think of quarterbacks and linebackers and sacks and touchdowns, but, to the rest of the world, football means soccer.

In the summer of 2002, my family and I traveled to Spain, and everywhere we went, the topic was World Cup. In hotel lobbies, in restaurants, in pubs, customers gathered around large TV screens to catch that day's action.

Here in the States, I had never been a soccer fan. I played all sorts of sports with my friends—basketball, football, and baseball mostly—but I had never played soccer even once. With the game having low scores like 1–0 and 2–1, I found myself wondering where the excitement might lie.

So I was kind of surprised when I surrendered to the enthusiasm of all those Spanish football fans. The more I watched, the more I enjoyed the game. The more I talked with the other fans, the more I learned about football's intricacies. By the time the vacation drew to a close, I was adjusting my schedule around that day's afternoon and evening telecasts. Fortunately, my parents didn't give me too hard a time about not joining them for their typical tourist stuff.

Now, six years later, I still haven't played a minute of soccer, but I do consider myself an expert in the sport. For one thing, I've watched lots of soccer on TV. Just recently I purchased a special soccer cable package that gives me access to just about every major game in the world. The second thing is FIFA 2007, the latest version of the world's best football video game.

You may know that there are two ways you can play this game: you can play against the computer or against a human opponent. When I go against the computer, I win nineteen out of twenty. Against another person I do almost as well: sixteen out of twenty.

My success is due to three factors: practice, patience, and strategy. I practice about two hours a week. That may not seem like very much, but if you consider that each game takes about twenty minutes, that means that I play around six games a week.

Patience is needed because in football you just can't rush things. You have to wait for a play to develop. It's a little like Wayne Gretzky, the ice hockey immortal. Gretzky was enormously skilled but not especially fast, so he just kind of waited for the action to rush past him, and then he'd be left to do his thing.

Strategy is mostly a matter of choosing the formation that suits the skills of your players. In order to do that well, you need to know your players' strengths and weaknesses.

There's a big difference between playing against a computer and playing against another person. After playing against the computer, I found that I learned to adjust to the computer's tendencies. Against a live opponent, you never know what to expect. People are unpredictable.

As I said, I've never played soccer on any level, but that's not a problem. I think it's interesting how you can learn to understand a sport just by watching it.

OK, nice speech, right? Matt takes his seat to polite applause and a few high-fives. When the class again settles, the teacher asks this question: "I'd like you to write a good paragraph about some of the important steps Matt has taken to develop his interest."

You're thinking, "Piece of cake!" because your notes look like this:

Matt & FIFA

- football = soccer
- 2002—Spain, World Cup
- low scores, but much enthusiasm
- FIFA 2007—comp (19/20) or human (16/20) opp
- 3 factors => success: practice, patience, strategy
- 2 hrs = 6 gms
- Gretz
- formation—skills—stren/weak
- comp predictable, human not
- watching, not playing

You have noticed that these brief notes include some of the aforementioned strategies. The note-taker has supplied a title, included important details and ideas, and used appropriate symbols and abbreviations. For sure, some of this shorthand is personal and spontaneous.

The resulting paragraph would probably focus on Matt's eye-opening trip to Spain, during which he first cultivated an interest in soccer, or it could describe how "practice, patience, and strategy" have enabled him to become a superior FIFA 2007 player. Either way, your notes have set you up for success.

BRAIN TICKLER
Set #27

While you listen to the following passage on the life of the urban artist Jean-Michel Basquiat, take careful notes. (It would certainly help if you could ask someone to read the passage to you, so that you can really get the experience of taking notes while you listen.)

"Every Single Line Means Something": Jean-Michel Basquiat

Jean-Michel Basquiat was born in Brooklyn, New York, in 1960, to parents of Puerto Rican and Haitian descent. When he was a very young child, his mother noticed his ability to draw and paint, and she encouraged him to develop these abilities. Upon her urging, he frequently visited the Brooklyn Museum. Then, when he was eight years old, he was hospitalized because of an auto accident. To help him pass the time, his mother gave him a copy of *Gray's Anatomy*. He studied this text carefully and was inspired by the illustrations of human physiology.

When he was still a teenager, his artistic career took a strange turn: he began to spray-paint graffiti on buildings in downtown Manhattan. Until that time, defacing public or private property was considered merely an anti-social crime, but Basquiat showed that graffiti was art. Observers took note of his talent and in 1978 the *Village Voice* published an article about his work.

At about the same time Basquiat dropped out of high school and began to live independently with some friends in Manhattan. He managed to make some money by selling hand-painted tee shirts and postcards on the city's streets. Before long, however, Basquiat's reputation began to spread. He was known, naturally, for his increasingly diverse artwork, but also for his performances in a band called Gray. Within a few years, he became a celebrated figure in the New York art scene.

It's hard to describe Basquiat's style because that style changed over the years, but one thing's for sure: no one else painted quite as he did. Certainly his work shows his awareness of his Caribbean background and his racial identity. In his paintings Basquiat combined brilliant colors, shocking figures, and child-like brush strokes in an entirely unique way. His canvasses were funny and frightening and outrageous—and beautiful—all at the same time. There was something raw and urgent about his work, some quality that spoke to the artistic yearnings of young people. It's not surprising that famous artists like Julian Schnabel and Andy Warhol were eager to promote his career.

Unfortunately, Basquiat became involved with drugs, and he died of a drug overdose in 1988. He was only twenty-seven years old. He died before he could appreciate fully his impact on artists of his and future generations. And could he possibly have imagined that one of his paintings would sell in 2007 for more than $14 million? Saddest of all, who knows where this uncommonly talented artist might have directed his boundless energy?

OWNING THE TEXT

Reading is an *active* experience. This is especially so for good readers, who read carefully, closely, and critically.

- A careful reader remains focused on the text. He or she knows that attention is a prerequisite for understanding. Such a reader does not permit external stimuli, such as music, television, or friends, to break his or her concentration. A careful reader's attention may wander occasionally, but he or she will reread material, if necessary.
- A close reader recognizes the importance of words and images. If a close reader does not understand a particular word, he or she will use the context or a dictionary to discover the word's meaning. A close reader will reread a sentence (or a portion of a sentence) if he or she has not fully understood the material.
- A critical reader questions and evaluates as he or she reads. Such a reader thinks carefully about the facts and ideas that have been presented. A critical reader questions the writer's bias and the authority of facts and statements and wonders whether he or she should agree or disagree with the writer. A critical reader thinks about what has been included and what has been left out. He or she tries to anticipate the direction the writer will take. In these ways, a critical reader is, in effect, a step ahead of the writer.

Keep in mind that not all reading requires this degree of care. There's a big difference between recreational reading and study. After all, as you're skimming the sports pages, you realize that you probably don't need to remember Derek Jeter's exact batting average on July 23. However, if you are reading your social studies text and know that you can expect a quiz the next day, you should know, for example, that President Harry S. Truman ordered the use of nuclear weapons to bring World War II to an end.

BRAIN TICKLER
Set #28

Are you an active reader? Indicate the extent to which these statements describe your reading.

	Often	Sometimes	Rarely
I read in a quiet environment that is free from distractions.			
If my attention wanders, I reread the passage.			
If I don't know a word, I use the context or a dictionary.			
If I don't understand a sentence or passage, I reread the material.			
As I am reading, I question the author's biases and authority.			
As I am reading, I think about whether I agree or disagree with the author.			

So . . . when do you really need to take notes while reading? For the most part, that's a decision that you are going to have to make, but you may find that your note-taking needs fall into three categories:

1. Test and Quiz Preparation. Has your teacher ever said something like this: "Tonight please read the following pages in your text, and expect a quiz tomorrow"? If so, then you know that merely reading the material will not provide the best preparation. You also need to take good notes.

2. Reading Journals. This specialized activity is probably the least formal category of note-taking. Many English Language Arts teachers ask their students to maintain reading journals. For some students, this can be a difficult task. Good note-taking will help greatly.

3. Research. Your teachers will ask you to conduct formal research and to write different kinds of papers based on what you have learned. (A separate chapter in this book will consider in greater detail the entire research process; this chapter will focus only on note-taking.) Note-taking plays a central role in the research process.

Major Mistake Territory!

Some teachers encourage students to underline or highlight as they read. Why do teachers promote this practice? Well, they do so because they believe that a student who underlines or highlights is reading actively. The very act of underlining or highlighting, they would contend, implies that a student is making some critical judgments about which portions of the text are more important than others.

This may or may not be true, since some students have been known to underline or highlight huge sections—say, more than half—of a given reading. But even if it is true, underlining or highlighting simply does not go far enough—not nearly. Remember that note-taking is about owning the text, and the only way that you can do that is to take what you're reading and put it (or most of it, in any case) into your own words. Also, you can easily imagine that rereading a heavily or scantily underlined or highlighted passage is not the easiest or most productive way of learning the most important material.

TAKING NOTES FOR TEST AND QUIZ PREPARATION

Here's a typical assignment, one that you might receive from any of your teachers:

Due tomorrow: Read pages 137 to 141. Answer questions 1–4 on page 141.

Now, if you are a typical student, you know that the shortest distance between two points is a straight line. In other words, you are not going to turn to page 137 and read every word of the next four pages. No way! What you're going to do is this: you're going to open to page 141, read question #1, and find the portion of the text that will enable you to answer it. You will do the same for questions 2, 3, and 4, and the following day you will submit a completed assignment that earns your teacher's approval.

Sound familiar? If so, you may congratulate yourself for having developed a successful shortcut to academic success. However, if you are determined to take the next step in becoming a superior student, you are going to have to rethink that strategy.

Why? Because you've accomplished little more than completing your homework. And, while you're to be complimented for that, you also need to understand that you've done little in the way of studying. When your next test or quiz comes around, you're practically starting from scratch.

But here's the good news: taking notes from most textbooks is very easy. Textbooks have been written so that you *can* take notes very easily. They are written logically, organized into chapters, subchapters, sections, and paragraphs. There is in each chapter a movement from the general to the more specific. In most textbooks, the development and presentation of ideas are quite obvious. In fact, you will probably find that much of the conceptual work has already been done for you.

Let's say your health teacher has asked you to read a passage on cystic fibrosis and has told you that you can expect a quiz on this material. Here is the passage:

In the United States alone, about 30,000 children and adults have been diagnosed with cystic fibrosis, an inherited disease that affects the lungs and digestive systems. Because of a defective gene, the body of a person with CF produces thick mucus that can clog up the lungs and lead to life-threatening lung infections. This mucus can also affect the pancreas, preventing its enzymes from helping the body break down digested food.

Most new CF patients are diagnosed when they are very young. In fact, about 1,000 new CF cases are diagnosed every year. Way back in the 1950s, most children with CF did not reach adulthood, but today, thanks to research and medical treatments, many people with CF can expect to live into their thirties or beyond. The average life span of a person with CF is thirty-seven years.

People with CF typically exhibit a variety of symptoms. Most of these affect the pulmonary system. People with CF often suffer from persistent coughing and lung infections, experience a mucus-type drip in their throats, and suffer from wheezing and/or shortness of breath. Because of problems associated with the pancreas, sometimes they do not gain enough weight to keep up with age-related growth rates. Some people with CF experience difficulty with bowel movements.

Because of their respiratory difficulties, people with CF must practice airway clearance techniques in order to rid the lungs of mucus. Some of these techniques are mechanical. For example, a patient may be asked to blow into a device that helps shake the mucus loose. Some of the techniques involve using medicines that when inhaled in mist form will also help clear the lungs. Unfortunately, people with CF develop their share of lung infections and must depend upon antibiotics and other types of drugs. Good nutrition can also play a role in keeping CF patients healthy.

Sometimes people with CF can develop serious lung diseases, which jeopardize their lives. In such cases, lung transplantation is an option. However, lung transplantation is a very serious procedure, and many factors, such as the patient's overall physical health, emotional well-being, and support system, must be considered.

You've read the passage. It's straightforward, and it contains a lot of information. You have before you a clean sheet of looseleaf paper. The pen is cocked in your hand. The first question—the basic question of note-taking—is simply this: what do I need to know?

Look again at that first sentence: "In the United States alone, about 30,000 children and adults have been diagnosed with cystic fibrosis, an inherited disease that affects the lungs and digestive systems." In this sentence alone, you have three pieces of information, so you might jot down notes—in bullet form— that look something like this:

- U.S.: 30,000 diagnosed w/ CF
- inherited disease
- affects lungs, digestive system

Good start! Now consider the second sentence: "Because of a defective gene, the body of a person with CF produces thick mucus that can clog up the lungs and lead to life-threatening lung infections." You can see that some of the information in this sentence connects with information in the notes you've already recorded, so you might simply add to your existing notes in this manner:

- U.S.: 30,000 diagnosed w/ CF
- inherited disease—defective gene => thick mucus
- affects lungs, digestive system—clogged lungs => life-threatening infections

The third sentence explains how the buildup of mucus can imperil the pancreas, which is a vital organ in the digestive system. This information you could easily add to that third bullet.

The second paragraph adds new material, primarily about diagnosis and long-term prospects. Your notes for that paragraph could look like this:

- most diagnosed when young—1,000 new cases/yr
- 1950s—most die in childhood
- today, b/c of research, medical treatments, many live to 30+ (average: 37)

You can see that taking good notes on an informative passage like this one could easily fill a whole page. But the notes present information in a way that is concise and direct, and information presented this way is very easy to study.

BRAIN TICKLER
Set #29

Focus on the fourth paragraph of the cystic fibrosis article. Reread the paragraph and compile some notes in bullet form.

TAKING NOTES FOR READING JOURNALS

It is not uncommon for English teachers to ask students to maintain reading journals. In recent years, this practice has been adopted by teachers of other subjects, such as social studies, science, health, foreign language, and even physical education!

Although the assignment will vary from teacher to teacher and subject to subject, the basic premise is similar: a student reads a book or a series of articles and prepares a written response to what he or she has read. The response often consists of a summary, followed by a personal reaction or analysis.

For many students, this kind of open-ended task can be thorny. It's hard to read, say, thirty to fifty pages over the course of a few days and then produce a well-written, thoughtful journal entry.

And that's why it's essential to take notes! Only by noting important events, ideas, and passages while you read can you later reflect insightfully on what you have read.

While you are reading, keep in mind your journal goals. If, as mentioned above, you are expected to include a summary and a personal reaction, you will keep notes that will aid you in those tasks.

Let's take an example. Read the very first paragraph of Thornton Wilder's prize-winning novel, *The Bridge of San Luis Rey*:

Part One: Perhaps an Accident

On Friday noon, July the twentieth, 1714, the finest bridge in all Peru broke and precipitated five travelers into the gulf below. The bridge was on the high-road between Lima and Cuzco and hundreds of persons passed over it every day. It had been woven of osier by the Incas more than a century before and visitors to the city were always led out to see it. It was a mere ladder of thin slats swung out over the gorge, with handrails of dried vine. Horses and coaches and chairs had to go down hundreds of feet below and pass over the narrow torrent on rafts, but no one, not even the Viceroy, not even the Archbishop of Lima, had descended with the baggage rather than cross by the famous bridge of San Luis Rey. St. Louis of France himself protected it, by his name and by the little mud church on the farther side. The bridge seemed to be among the things that last forever; it was unthinkable that is should break. The moment a Peruvian heard of the accident he signed himself and made a mental calculation as to how recently he had crossed by it and how soon he had intended crossing by it again. People wandered about in a trance-like state, muttering; they had the hallucination of seeing themselves falling into a gulf.

As you read that first, rather lengthy paragraph, you ask yourself what events have taken place. There is only one event, but it is central to the novel: on July 20, 1714, the Bridge of San

Luis Rey, located in Peru, somehow broke, sending five travelers to their death. In terms of the novel's plot, this would probably be the only note you would record.

However, at the same time you make a couple of observations:

- Despite the fact that the bridge is a "mere ladder," it is considered to be quite marvelous, so much so that no one—tourists or high officials—refuses the opportunity to see it or travel over it.
- The bridge's destruction is "perhaps an accident," which is to say that perhaps it isn't. Despite the fact that people think the bridge unbreakable, despite the fact that the bridge is protected by the church, it breaks. It's only natural to wonder why.

Now you *might* record these observations in some briefer form. You could simply write "bridge marvelous" for the first and "perhaps an accident" for the second. You would also indicate the appropriate page numbers so you could return to these sections later on.

Or, at this point, you could write nothing. Sometimes a mental note will suffice. Keep these thematic guesses on the back burner until you gather some additional evidence.

In this novel, additional evidence will arrive soon. A few pages later the reader learns that Brother Juniper, a clergyman visiting from Italy, happens to witness the tragedy:

> *Anyone else would have said to himself with secret joy: "Within ten minutes myself . . . !" But it was another thought that visited Brother Juniper: "Why did this happen to those five?" If there were any plan in the universe at all, if there were any pattern in a human life, surely it could be discovered mysteriously latent [i.e., concealed] in those lives so suddenly cut off. Either we live by accident and die by accident, or we live by plan and die by plan. And on that instant Brother Juniper made the resolve to inquire into the secret lives of those five persons, that moment falling through the air, and to surprise [i.e., discover] the reason of their taking off.*

This section passage offers one important plot fact and, at the same time, confirmation of your thoughts about one of the novel's themes. Regarding the former, Brother Juniper decides to investigate the lives of the five victims of the tragedy. Regarding the latter, he will attempt to determine whether people's lives are or are not ruled by some master plan.

You are only a few pages into the novel, but already you have recorded a few notes:

- 7/20/1714—bridge collapses, 5 die
- bridge considered to be a marvel—tourists, high officials (3)
- "perhaps an accident"—Bro Juniper to investigate 5 lives, determine whether accident or divine plan (6)

Notice that two of the notes include page numbers.

And, even though you have not completed the first chapter, you can see the shape your journal entry might take. Your plot summary, should one be necessary, would be rather brief, because, plotwise, not much has happened. However, you already possess a solid grasp of one of the novel's central themes, and you can discuss it in some detail.

BRAIN TICKLER
Set #30

Read this passage, which comprises the last three paragraphs of the first chapter of *The Bridge of San Luis Rey*. While you are reading, take notes.

Thus it was that the determination rose within him [Brother Juniper] at the moment of the accident. It prompted him to busy himself for six years, knocking at all the doors in Lima, asking thousands of questions, filling scores of notebooks, in his effort at establishing the fact that each of the five lost lives was a perfect whole. Everyone knew that he was working on some sort of memorial of the accident and everyone was very

*helpful and misleading. A few even
knew the principal aim of his activity
and there were patrons in high places.*

*The result of all this diligence was
an enormous book, which, as we shall
see later, was publicly burned on a
beautiful Spring morning in the great
square. But there was a secret copy
and after a great many years and
without much notice it found its way
to the library at the University of San
Marco. There it lies between two great
wooden covers collecting dust in a cup-
board. It deals with one after another
of the victims of the accident, catalogu-
ing thousands of little facts and anec-
dotes and testimonies, and concluding with a dignified
passage describing why God had settled upon that person
and upon that day for His demonstration of wisdom. Yet
for all his diligence Brother Juniper never knew the central
passion of Dona Maria's life; nor of Uncle Pio's, not even of
Esteban's. And I, who claim to know so much more, isn't it
possible that even I have missed the very spring with the
spring?*

*Some say that we shall never know that to the gods we
are like flies that the boys kill on a summer day, and some
say, on the contrary, that the very sparrows do not lose a
feather that has not been brushed away by the finger of God.*

TAKING NOTES FOR RESEARCH

Let's assume that your entire grade is participating in an
interdisciplinary project called the Great Debate. Groups of
students have been assigned separate topics, and each person's
task is to conduct research on the topic and to prepare and
deliver a speech on the information that person has acquired.
You have been assigned to the "Capital Punishment (Opposed)"
group. You and your teammates have discussed the topic, and
you have been given the subtopic of "DNA evidence."

When you visit the library, your helpful librarian hands you a folder filled with articles (she has evidently done her homework), so you know that finding suitable material will not be a problem.

The first article you come across is entitled, "DNA Evidence Exonerates Louisiana Death Row Inmate," and you think this should be useful. Your first step is to read the article in its entirety to make sure you are correct.

When Ryan Matthews was seventeen years old, he was arrested in Bridge City, Louisiana, for the murder of a grocery store owner. Witnesses reported that a single masked gunman entered the store, demanded money of the owner, and, when the owner refused, shot him and fled. The gunman removed his ski mask and left it at the scene. One of the witnesses handed it to the police.

Ryan knew he was not that gunman.

Three witnesses were not able to identify Matthews with any degree of certainty. They said that the gunman was only about 5'8" tall, whereas Matthews is over six feet. Also, the defense attorney, appointed by the court, was not able to handle the DNA evidence, which was not presented during the trial.

So why was Matthews even arrested? Witnesses claimed that, after discarding his mask, the gunman jumped into a getaway car. Hours later, Matthews was found in a vehicle resembling the one reportedly identified at the crime scene.

*The trial lasted only three days. It seemed to some ob-
servers that the judge was trying to rush things along. On
the second day, for example, at 10:00 P.M., he first ordered
both sides to begin their final arguments. On the third day,
the jury could not agree upon a verdict, but the judge said
that they should continue their deliberations until they did.
Two hours later, they came back with a guilty verdict, and
Matthews was sentenced to death.*

*In March 2003 Matthews' new lawyers arranged for the
DNA evidence to be retested. The lab examined saliva and
skin cells found on the ski mask and concluded that
Matthews could not have committed the crime. In fact, the
DNA evidence pointed to another person who was already
serving time for another murder committed a few months
after the one for which Matthews was charged and convicted. This person eventually confessed to the crime.*

*On August 9, 2004, Jefferson Parish prosecutors
dropped all charges against Matthews. He was released into
his mother's care.*

"Excellent article!" you correctly conclude, and your next
step is to create a source card. In order to get started, you will
need a stack of 3" × 5" index cards, lined on one side. These you
will use for source cards and note cards.

Later in this book, you will learn a great deal more about
source cards and citations. For now, it is enough for you to know
that every source you consult gets its own source card on which
you will record all necessary information about that source. This
way, when you need to consult the source again or compile a
Works Cited sheet, you have all the information you need.

You will also assign a number to each source. This number
you will write in the upper right-hand corner of the source card.
Most important, you will write that same number on every note
card corresponding to that source. For example, if you compile
eight note cards for source #1, each of those note cards will have
the numeral "1" written in the upper right-hand corner.

Let's assume that the Ryan Matthews article is the first you
read. Let's further assume that you have already completed a
source card for the article and that you have identified it as
source #1.

Before you write some note cards, you need to consider a few general principles:

1. You may **summarize** important information. When you summarize, you take a great deal of information, and you put it in your own words. A summary is much briefer than the material it summarizes.

2. You may **paraphrase** important information. When you paraphrase, you take a smaller piece of information, and you put it in your own words. Essentially, you are restating the author's words in your own.

3. You may **directly quote** information. When you directly quote information, you copy exactly what the author has to say. You choose to use the author's words instead of your own because the author has used language that you cannot paraphrase or summarize without diminishing the impact of his words. Use direct quotes selectively, and try to keep your quotes short. Remember to use quotation marks to indicate that you have quoted directly.

4. Include the number of the page or pages where you found your information. Write **page numbers** in parentheses at the end of the note.

5. Give each note card a brief **title**. This will give you a quick idea of the card's contents.

6. Keep your notes **brief**. Try not to include too much information on one card. In fact, some teachers teach their students to write only one note (that is, one single item of information) per card. You may find this is a good way to start taking notes.

Major Mistake Territory!

By now you have undoubtedly heard the word *plagiarism*. This word refers to the practice of passing off someone else's ideas or words as your own. In schools and in professional circles, plagiarism is considered a very serious offense, which can result in a failing grade or even expulsion.

But don't be fooled! When your teachers warn you about plagiarizing, they are not telling you not to use another writer's words or ideas. After all, research is largely about using other people's words and ideas to help you build and support your own ideas! Your teachers are warning you about the danger of misrepresenting your own efforts. If you take proper notes and document your sources, you will avoid this kind of problem.

Let's get back to the Matthew's article. Having read it, you know that a crime has been committed and that someone was falsely accused and convicted of that crime. You also know that, thanks to DNA evidence, Ryan Matthews's conviction was eventually overturned and he was set free.

So your first card might focus on facts pertaining to the crime itself. This card could look like this:

1

The Crime

- Bridge City, La.
- masked gunman wanted $
- owner refused, shot
- gunman removed ski mask, fled
- getaway car

(95–96)

First of all, notice that the note card is numbered to indicate that this information comes from source #1. Second, the card contains a simple title. Most important, the bulleted information is simple and concise. Finally, notice the page numbers written in the lower right-hand corner of the card.

A second card could contain information about Matthews's arrest and conviction. It could very well look like this:

1

Matthews's Arrest and Conviction

- RM later found in car resembling getaway
- witnesses can't ID RM (5'8" not 6')
- court-appointed atty can't handle DNA (not used)
- hurried trial—3 days
- 2nd day—judge orders final arguments at 10 pm!
- 3rd day—judge orders jury to continue delibs
- RM guilty, sentenced to death

(96–97)

Notice that the second card is also numbered "1" so that you know that the information has been taken from your first source. This card contains a useful title. One way it differs from the first is that it makes greater use of abbreviations, such as "RM" for "Ryan Matthews" and "atty" for "attorney." Again, page numbers are indicated for easy reference.

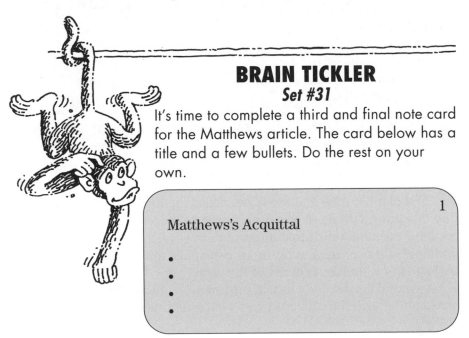

BRAIN TICKLER
Set #31

It's time to complete a third and final note card for the Matthews article. The card below has a title and a few bullets. Do the rest on your own.

1

Matthews's Acquittal

-
-
-
-

You will have noticed that the sample note cards do not contain a single example of direct quotation. Why? Because the article is written plainly and directly, and the information within the article is easily summarized and/or paraphrased.

ANNOTATING

Remember that for most of your education, the idea of taking notes meant copying from the board just what the teacher had already written. That's not exactly brain surgery, right? This chapter has focused instead on *independent* note-taking.

Well, there's a half-way point between copying notes and creating them independently, and that's where annotating comes in.

If you examine the word *annotate*, you will see *note* stuck right in the middle, and that's because *annotate* means "to take notes on."

Sometimes in your classes you will be given handouts that capture for you the material you need to know. Perhaps these handouts will already be in note or outline form. Or sometimes, as we said, you will be asked to copy notes or outlines from the board. The two activities pretty much amount to the same thing, since in both cases the work is delivered to you. Annotating differs slightly: when you annotate, you simply comment upon the material that has already been presented.

Let's take a look at a typical math problem.

Lee and his parents had dinner at a nearby restaurant. The bill came to $62.50. Because he enjoyed the food and the service, Lee suggested that they leave a 20% tip. The total cost of the meal came to

A. $62.50
B. $65.00
C. $72.50
D. $75.00

Your class discussed the problem. One student said he would multiply the cost of the meal, $62.50, by 0.2, the decimal equivalent of 20%, and then add that amount to $62.50. Another suggested a quicker route. Instead of adding the tip to the food bill, she would multiply $62.50 by 1.2. The teacher said each solution would work. The board work looked like this:

$$
\begin{array}{r}
62.5 \\
\times\ 1.2 \\
\hline
1250 \\
625 \\
\hline
75.00
\end{array}
$$

That's easy enough, right? The correct answer is D. And it would certainly be very easy for you to copy that solution directly into your notes or on to your worksheet. However, you are aware of your purpose: you know that you are copying this material mostly for future reference. If you want this particular problem to help you solve similar ones, you need to take the next step: annotate. Here's what that would look like:

$$
\begin{array}{r}
62.5 \\
\times\ 1.2 \\
\hline
1250 \\
625 \\
\hline
75.00
\end{array}
$$
→ (Mult. by 1 (the cost of the meal) and 0.2 (the tip—20%))

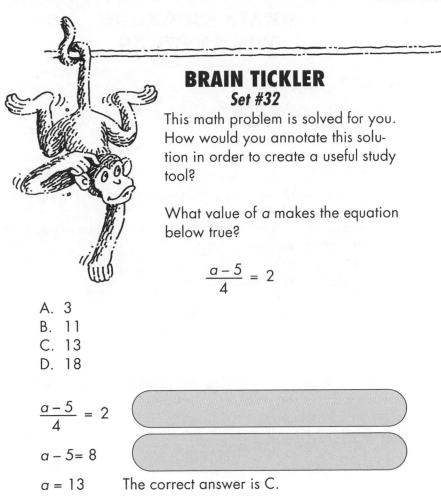

BRAIN TICKLER
Set #32

This math problem is solved for you. How would you annotate this solution in order to create a useful study tool?

What value of a makes the equation below true?

$$\frac{a-5}{4} = 2$$

A. 3
B. 11
C. 13
D. 18

$$\frac{a-5}{4} = 2$$

$$a - 5 = 8$$

$$a = 13$$ The correct answer is C.

Remember that the whole idea of note-taking is ownership. Whether you are taking notes in your head, preparing for a reading journal, reading an article for research, or annotating a math problem, you are taking firm hold of that material and making it yours. It's a huge step toward becoming a superior student.

BRAIN TICKLERS
THE ANSWERS

Set #23, page 77

Answers will vary, but here is an admittedly incomplete list:

- During telephone conversations
- Preparing a shopping list
- Recording driving directions
- During group and individual (one-on-one) staff meetings
- Purchasing a product
- Preparing for a job interview (or an interview of any kind)
- Recording a recipe
- During lectures
- Preparing presentations for work
- Writing speeches
- During parent-teacher conferences

Set #24, page 79

Answers will vary. Characteristics of good listeners will be discussed within the text.

Set #25, page 82

Answers will vary.

Set #26, page 84

1. c
2. g
3. e
4. h
5. a

6. j
7. i
8. d
9. f
10. b

Set #27, page 87

Answers will vary, of course, but your notes might resemble these:

Jean-Michel Basquiat

- bn Bklyn, 1960, parents Haiti/PR
- mom helps: Bklyn Mus, auto acc=>Gray's Anat
- teen: graffiti on Man bldgs, graf as art, Vill Voice article
- drops out, lives w/ friends in Man
- sells painted t-shirts, postcds
- band Gray
- style: Carib bkgd, racial ID/bril colors, shock fig, ch-like brush strokes
- raw, urgent—connected w/ young
- helped by artists Warhol, Schnabel
- drugs=>death, 1988: didn't know impact on artists, value of paintings ($14 mil), or what he might have done

Set #28, page 90

Answers will vary.

Set #29, 95

Answers will vary, but the notes could look like these:

- airway clearance techniques—mechanical (e.g., blow into device) or medicinal (inhaled mist)
- antibiotics for infections
- good nutrition important

Set #30, page 98

Answers will vary, but the notes could look like these:

- Brother Juniper: 6 yrs of research
- "everyone was helpful and misleading" (8)
- book burned, but secret copy
- what's missing: "central passion" (8)
- differing opinions about role of divine being (see last para, 9!)

You can see that the first three notes comment on plot developments, whereas the last two address what appear to be important thematic elements in the novel. Note also that three of the notes include page numbers because the author's language is itself quite revealing and because you might want to return to those sections of the text.

Set #31, page 104

Answers will vary, but the card could look like this:

1

1

Matthews's Acquittal

- 3/03: RM's attys have DNA retested
- ski mask (saliva, skin cells) show another committed crime
- convicted of 2nd murder, real killer confesses
- 8/9/04: Jefferson Parish drops charges

(97)

Set #32, page 107

Answers will vary.

$$\frac{a-5}{4} = 2$$

Multiply both sides of the equation by 4. It's like solving a proportion.

$$a - 5 = 8$$

Add 5 to both sides of the equation.

$$a = 13$$

CHAPTER FIVE

Creating Wonderful Outlines

I.   Factors
    A. prime numbers
    B. prime factorization
    C. greatest common factor
       1. relatively prime
       2. monomials
II. Fractions
    A. equivalent fractions
       1. fractions in simplest form
       2. simplifying a variable
       3. solving problems
    B. least common multiple
       1. monomials
       2. comparing fractions using
    the least common denominator

THE DIFFERENCE BETWEEN NOTES AND OUTLINES

On the one hand, you have this raw product: your notes. On the other hand, you can see some final product in the not-too-distant future: a really high grade on a test, a splendid research paper.

An outline is that in-between step, the one that will help lead you from raw to finished product.

Outlines serve two essential purposes. One is to help you prepare for tests, quizzes, and presentations. The second is to help you prepare for major writing tasks, such as essays, articles, or research papers.

What exactly is an outline? An outline is an organizational plan. It does for facts and details what a blueprint does for space. It turns chaos into order.

Imagine that you're headed to the supermarket with a relatively long list of items that you need to pick up. Your list could look like this:

- whole milk
- filet of sole
- ½ lb boiled ham
- iceberg lettuce
- ½ lb swiss cheese sliced
- 1 lb ground sirloin
- Macintosh apples
- paper towels
- grape juice
- sliced bread
- Raisin Bran
- half and half
- aged Comte cheese
- carrots
- granola
- string beans
- orange juice
- chicken cut up in ⅛ ths
- tomatoes
- oatmeal
- olive oil
- Kleenex tissues
- 1 lb coffee
- yogurts
- 6 bagels
- blueberries
- sodas
- waffles

Such a list would undoubtedly be useful, but, knowing the way your supermarket is organized, you might be able to do a little better. You could put together a list that would look like this:

Produce	Dairy	Meats	Frozen Foods	Drinks	Appetizing	Other
iceberg lettuce	whole milk	filet of sole	waffles	soda	½ lb boiled ham	paper towels
Mac apples	yogurts	1 lb ground sirloin	6 bagels	grape juice	½ lb swiss chesse	sliced bread
carrots	half and half	chicken cut up				Raisin Bran
string beans	Comte cheese					granola
tomatoes	orange juice					oatmeal
blueberries						olive oil
						Kleenex tissues
						1 lb coffee

A shopping list like the one above organizes your shopping needs according to where you might find these articles in the aisles or sections of your favorite supermarket. Using it will save you time when you try to look for various articles and later, having found them, cross them off your list.

This is exactly what outlines do. They organize things—ideas, facts, concepts, details—by placing them in the proper category.

OUTLINES THAT ORGANIZE

If you think of an outline as an organization plan—as some attempt to group and organize related information—you will not get too stuffy about what is or isn't an outline. The point is that outlines don't have to be very formal. Some are, but others are not.

Let's say that your teacher wants you to read Guy de Maupassant's short story "The Necklace" and write a good body paragraph about the author's use of foreshadowing. You know what foreshadowing means: the technique of giving the reader hints of what is to come. And you also know how the story ends: the necklace that Mathilde Loisel borrowed, lost, and replaced (at great cost) was made of false diamonds. So your next step is to re-read the story and, as you do so, create an informal outline that looks like this:

EXAMPLES OF FORESHADOWING IN "THE NECKLACE"

Example	Explanation
Madame Forestier lends her the necklace without making a big deal over it.	It's very unusual for even a good friend to lend something of such great value.
The jeweler claims that his store only supplied the box, not the necklace.	It could mean that an inexpensive necklace was placed inside a box from another store.

This "outline" more closely resembles a traditional graphic organizer than what we will refer to as a Harvard outline. It may be informal, but it does the trick: it offers all the information you will need to write that paragraph well.

BRAIN TICKLER
Set #33

Read the poem below. Prepare a graphic organizer that will help you to discuss the ways in which the poem's first stanza is similar to and different from the second.

Oh, when I was in love with you,
Then I was clean and brave,
And miles around the wonder grew
How well did I behave.

And now the fancy passes by,
And nothing will remain,
And miles around they'll say that I
Am quite myself again.
—A. E. Housman

So there's nothing wrong with using a graphic organizer for informal outlining purposes. However, if you are dealing with a more comprehensive task, you may need to resort to a more formal outline: this is sometimes called a Harvard outline.

Let's return for a while to your hypothetical English class and this hypothetical class discussion of de Maupassant's "The Necklace." The class has enjoyed the story's surprise ending—Mathilde Loisel's discovery that the necklace is false—but now your teacher wants the class to think about why the story's surprise ending is so successful. After examining the story very closely, the class might very well produce an outline that looks like this:

Why the Ending of "The Necklace" Succeeds

I. Foreshadowing sets up surprise ending

    A. Mme. Forestier lends Mathilde "expensive" necklace

    B. Jeweler provided casket only

II. Small ironies prepare reader for bigger irony

    A. Mme. Forestier owns a fake necklace

        1. A rich person expected to own real diamonds

        2. Mme. F: a fake herself?

    B. Mathilde's sensational first night at the party is also her last night as a social success

        1. She is the hit of the ball

        2. Repaying their debts, she has neither time, money, nor beauty for partying

    C. With great pride Mathilde tells Mme. Forestier how she replaced the necklace

III. Point of view preserves element of surprise

    A. Third person limited omniscient—only through Mathilde's eyes

    B. Reader never learns what others (especially Mme. Forestier) are thinking

Notice, first of all, that the outline contains a title. All outlines—formal or informal—should do so. Second, merely by looking at the Roman numerals, you can tell that the outline contains three main ideas. The first is the use of foreshadowing, the second is the use of small ironies, and the third is the use of a particular point of view. The capital letters within each of these main ideas shows you that they are developed with some detail. Two of these "capital letter" details are themselves developed in greater detail, and this is shown by the use of standard numerals.

Such an outline serves as a good study tool or a writing plan.

BRAIN TICKLER
Set #34

Read "The Monkey's Paw," a famous short story by W. W. Jacobs. (It can be found in any library or online.) Prepare an outline that examines the story's plot by taking a close look at its conflicts, crisis (climax), and resolution.

PREPARING OUTLINES FROM TEXTBOOK READINGS

Throughout your secondary educational career, you will be asked to read portions of many textbooks, and you will be held accountable for what you read.

You can listen to your favorite song over and over again. A great movie like *The Godfather* can certainly stand up to multiple viewings. TV networks make a lot of money because people don't seem to mind watching reruns of their favorite shows (*Seinfeld*, anyone?). If you have an absolute favorite novel (Sue Hinton's *The Outsiders*, for example), you may very well have read it a second or even a third time.

But let's face it: most of the textbooks you will have to read will not fall into those categories. They may be fairly well-written, and they are certainly informative, but no one wants to read them twice. Why read a chapter once, when you're doing homework, and then read it again, when you're about to study for a test?

That's why it's imperative that you learn to create good outlines from textbook readings.

Here's the really good news: it's very easy to do so. First of all, textbook chapters can be very easily converted to good outlines. Second, you can omit a separate note-taking stage. In other words, you don't have to read, take notes, and then create an outline. You can just skip that second step.

To illustrate just how easy this process can be, let's take a look at any American history textbook. Turn to the Table of Contents and locate the chapter on World War I. (If you don't have a textbook handy, any encyclopedia—hard copy or online—will serve just as well.) Find the beginning of that chapter.

You might find on the very first page of the chapter some kind of chapter outline, which will tell you precisely how that chapter is organized. It could look like this:

Chapter Outline

    I. The War Begins in Europe

   II. The United States Enters the War

 III. A Brutal Year of Battle

 IV. President Wilson Builds the Peace

Just by glancing at this page, you already have a pretty good idea how your outline will be constructed: it will have a title (probably "World War I"), and you see just what your Roman numeral topics will be.

Flip the page. You know that the first section of this chapter will discuss the war in Europe. As you examine the first pages of the chapter (or, for that matter, the first pages of *any* chapter), you will see how the author uses clues to divide each section into subsections and sub-subsections. What clues does the author provide? Here are a few:

- page breaks
- different fonts, font sizes, and font styles (that is, bold, italics, underlining)
- capitalization
- ink colors

Using these clues, you might discover that the first section, "The War Begins in Europe," is divided into these three sub-sections:

- Tensions Build in Europe
- The War Begins
- America Remains Neutral

You can already see your outline taking a more detailed shape:

World War I

   I. The War Begins in Europe

      A. Tensions Build in Europe

      B. The War Begins

      C. America Remains Neutral

  II. The United States Enters the War

 III. A Brutal Year of Battle

 IV. President Wilson Builds the Peace

Now you're ready to find out just how tensions began to build in Europe. Again, a quick look at section headings reveals three separate factors: nationalism, imperialism, and alliances. You can see that these will form the "1," "2," and "3" below I.A.:

   I. The War Begins in Europe

      A. Tensions Build in Europe

         1. Nationalism

         2. Imperialism

         3. Rival alliances

OK, it looks good so far, but you really haven't even taken a close look at the text. So, as you read, you will take notes—and now you know precisely where to place them.

I. The War Begins in Europe

  A. Tensions Build in Europe

    1. Nationalism

      a. Def: people w/ same culture want to govern themselves

      b. One nation opposes another

      c. Germany takes Alsace-Lorraine from France

      d. Russia encourages Serbs to oppose rulers in Austria-Hungary

    2. Imperialism

      a. Def: desire to extend rule over other countries, often for economic reasons

      b. England, Germany, Italy, France, and Russia compete for colonies in Africa and Asia

    3. Rival alliances

      a. Militarism: countries build strong armies to prepare for war (e.g., Germany's naval expansion => Britain's)

      b. Form for mutual protection

        (1) Triple Alliance = Germany, Italy, and Austria-Hungary

        (2) Triple Entente = France, England, Russia

As you continue your reading, you will provide comparable information for "B. The War Begins" and "C. America Remains Neutral." In this way, you create structure, of course, but, more important, you supply the information you will need to know.

BRAIN TICKLER
Set #35

In fact, skip down to that "C." Consult your textbook (or an encyclopedia) and create an outline that explains America's decision to remain neutral during the first few years of World War I.

CREATING OUTLINES FROM NOTES

When it comes to creating outlines, textbooks will do a lot of the work for you. Without the benefit of a textbook, you're more or less on your own. That's by no means an insurmountable problem. In fact, creating organization can be an intellectually satisfying task.

Once again, an outline is not your end product. You have gathered information (that is, notes), perhaps from more than one source, and now your goal is to present that information in some kind of easily understood format. Perhaps you will be delivering a speech to your class. Maybe you are writing an essay or a research paper. Regardless, once you have created an outline, you can clearly see exactly where you're headed.

Major Mistake Territory!

You will not always be given the time to create a detailed outline. For example, if you're taking a timed state assessment, and you know you only have forty-five minutes to answer three short-answer questions and an extended response, you might pass on the opportunity to write a complete outline. Even under these stressful conditions, try your best to plan *something*, even if it's just an informal attempt.

Most of the time, however, you will be given enough time to create an effective outline. What you need to understand is that an outline is a huge time-saving device. The time that you spend creating an outline will save you much more time later, when you actually do the required writing. Not only that: writing an outline beforehand makes all the rest of the work much easier.

So don't get lazy about outlines!

Here's a situation in which an outline surely would come in handy:

Your English class has been reading a novel, *Jim the Boy*, by Tony Earley. (Have you read it? It's a terrific book!) The novel is set in rural North Carolina in the 1930s, and your teacher wants the class to gather some background information pertaining to the events in the novel.

The novel's main character, Jim Glass, is both the best friend and rival of another boy, Penn Carson. At one point, the boys are having a catch, both trying to show off before Ty Cobb, a baseball star of that day, who happens to be passing through their town on a train. However, only Jim has a glove. Penn urges him to let him use it. Jim refuses, and the scene just gets uglier . . . until Penn mysteriously collapses and cannot move his legs.

Your teacher wants you to get some information about the baseball player Ty Cobb. What kind of man was he? What kind of baseball player was he? Why would the boys have tried so hard to make a favorable impression upon him?

Getting the information will not be difficult. Your school library should have several books on the subject, and of course you are welcome to use the Internet.

After a few periods of research, you think you have the information you need, and you've recorded that information (each bulleted item would have its own note cards), as follows:

- Born in Royston, Georgia—nicknamed "The Georgia Peach"
- Career batting average of .367 (highest ever)
- Scored 2,245 runs (most ever)
- 4,191 hits (most until broken by Pete Rose in 1980s)
- 1936—1st player inducted into Hall of Fame
- Father did not want him to play baseball—thought he'd become drunken womanizer—but told him, "Don't come home a failure"
- Cobb's father accidentally (?) shot by his mother—controversial incident
- Cobb learns quickly during his rookie season: slides headfirst on stolen base attempt, only to have opponent dig his knees in Cobb's back; thereafter, always slides feet first, and aggressively
- Despite some early problems, Cobb became a great outfielder, aggressively attacking the ball and often throwing out baserunners
- As a hitter, Cobb practiced constantly
- As a left-handed batter, Cobb learned to hit lefty pitchers to the opposite field
- Brought a vicious attitude to the plate: wanted to humiliate opposing pitcher
- Clever hitter: realized that flame-throwing Walter Johnson would not want to hit him w/ pitch, so he dug in, Johnson pitched him outside, and Cobb hit to left
- On bases, always ran hard: believed basepaths belonged to him
- Sometimes went from first to third base on a sacrifice bunt!
- Used his spikes to gain advantage (Philadelphia manager Connie Mack called him "the dirtiest player ever")
- Rumored that Cobb sharpened his spikes—he did not, but he enjoyed the psychological advantage this gave him
- Cobb did not get along with his teammates
- Some teammates feared that he would take their jobs (he did); some thought he was conceited (he was just quiet)
- Quarrels with teammates sometimes turned to fistfights, and Cobb took to sleeping with a gun

- Conflicts with opponents were even worse: e.g., during spring training in 1917, he slid hard into second base, was tagged with ball, and fought with a player from the New York Giants; continued fight back at the hotel
- Cobb was known as a racist—once charged the stands to fight with man who said he was of mixed race
- Retired after 1928 season as baseball's 1st millionaire
- Invested his money wisely, and his fortune grew
- Divorced twice; lonely old age when his sons' deaths preceded his
- Died from various illnesses in 1961

That's not bad, right? You've managed to come up with twenty-six separate note cards.

You've got a title for your outline: Ty Cobb, Baseball Immortal. That's easy enough.

Now, in order to get that outline going, you have to think of grouping pieces of information.

You might have a Roman numeral for a section called "Lifetime Achievements," and under that heading, you would place pertinent notes. It might look like this:

Ty Cobb, Baseball Immortal

I. Lifetime Achievements

    A. Career batter average of .367 (highest ever)

    B. Scored 2,245 runs (most ever)

    C. 4,191 hits most until broken by Pete Rose in 1980s

    D. 1936—1st player inducted into Hall of Fame

Once again, easy enough. What would be your next Roman numeral? Maybe you would be thinking about Cobb's childhood and family life. Thus, your next section could look like this:

II. Childhood and Family Life

    A. Father did not want him to play baseball (thought he'd become drunken womanizer)

    B. Father told Cobb, "Don't come home a failure"

    C. Cobb's father accidentally (?) shot by his mother—controversial incident

What would be your next main category or Roman numeral? It looks like there might be only two left, Cobb's Major League Career, and Life After Baseball. Let's finish off the outline.

III. Cobb's Major League Career

    A. Rookie season: Cobb learns quickly—slides headfirst on stolen base attempt, only to have opponent dig his knees in Cobb's back; thereafter, always slides feet first, and aggressively

    B. Fielding: despite some early problems Cobb became a great outfielder, aggressively attacking the ball and often throwing out baserunners

    C. Hitting

        1. Cobb practiced constantly

        2. As a left-handed batter, Cobb learned to hit lefty pitchers to the opposite field

        3. Brought a vicious attitude to the plate: wanted to humiliate opposing pitcher

        4. Clever hitter: realized that flame-throwing Walter Johnson would not want to hit him w/ pitch, so he dug in, Johnson pitched him outside, and Cobb hit to left

    D. Base running

        1. Always ran hard: believed basepaths belonged to him

        2. Sometimes went from first to third base on a sacrifice bunt!

        3. Used his spikes to gain advantage (Philadelphia manager Connie Mack called him "the dirtiest player ever")

        4. Rumored that Cobb sharpened his spikes—he did not, but he enjoyed the psychological advantage this gave him

    E. Relationships with other players

        1. Did not get along with teammates

        2. Some teammates feared that he would take their jobs (he did); some thought he was conceited (he was just quiet)

3. Quarrels with teammates sometimes turned to fistfights, and Cobb took to sleeping with a gun

4. Conflicts w/ opponents were even worse: e.g., during spring training in 1918, he slid hard into 2nd base, was tagged with ball, and fought with a player from the New York Giants; continued fight back at hotel

5. Cobb known as a racist—once charged the stands to fight with man who said he was of mixed race

IV. Life after baseball

   A. Retired after 1928 season as baseball's 1st millionaire

   B. Invested his money wisely, and his fortune grew

   C. Divorced twice; lonely old age when his sons' deaths preceded his

   D. Died from various illnesses in 1961

This activity should clarify for you the key activity that turns notes into outlines: it's all about grouping facts.

BRAIN TICKLER
Set #36

Roy Campanella is another famous American baseball player. The Los Angeles Dodgers give a Roy Campanella Award to the player who best exemplifies Campy's spirit and leadership. Consult some print and/or online sources. Find out why the Dodgers named this award after Campanella. Using Roman numerals only, create an outline that you could use for an oral report on Campanella's life.

PREPARING AN OUTLINE FOR A GENERAL WRITING TASK

These same principles of outlining apply to general writing assignments. A goal of nearly every secondary education writing program is the essay or composition. In order to write a good essay, you need to be able to prepare a good outline.

You know that an essay consists of three sections: an introduction, a body, and a conclusion. Chapter 7 will discuss some key points about essay writing, but for now, you need know only that you should not have to prepare an outline for the introduction or the conclusion. Prepare an outline only for the body of the essay. The reasons for this are quite simple. First of all, writing introductions and conclusions should become formulaic for you. Second, you can't really create an introduction or conclusion until you know what you're going to say in the body.

With that in mind, consider this second principle: each Roman numeral of your outline should correspond to a body paragraph. In other words, if you employ in your outline Roman numerals I, II, and III, that means that you will have only three body paragraphs.

You can take that a step further: each Roman numeral should give you a pretty good idea of what your topic sentence will be for that body paragraph. And all the material contained within that Roman numeral will furnish the details of that paragraph.

Let's say that your physical education teacher has assigned you an essay on the topic of sportsmanship. She has stipulated that you choose a sport that you have played and discuss what you have learned about sportsmanship in that particular sport.

Because basketball is by far your favorite game, the choice is easy.

You think about your experiences on the court, and you come away with this conclusion: poor sportsmanship usually shows itself in two ways, the verbal and the physical. Then it occurs to you that you may as well discuss good

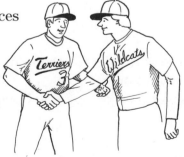

and bad sportsmanship as they pertain to each. So your outline's "bones" could look like this:

Sportsmanship in Basketball
  I. Physical
     A. Poor Sportsmanship
     B. Proper Sportsmanship
  II. Verbal
     A. Poor Sportsmanship
     B. Proper Sportsmanship

   At this point, you can tell that completing this outline will be easy. Why? Because you have the knowledge right at your fingertips. Here's a completed outline:

  I. Physical
     A. Poor Sportsmanship = Excessive Aggression
        1. Fouls that are too hard
        2. Intentionally trying to injure another, usually out of frustration
     B. Proper Sportsmanship = Restraint
        1. 100% effort can include physical play, but within the rules
        2. Develop "time-out" strategy if you think you're in danger of losing composure
  II. Verbal
     A. Poor Sportsmanship: taunting ("trash talk")
        1. Personal remarks
        2. Boasting
        3. Attempts to disrupt opponent's concentration
        4. Mocking an opponent's failure
     B. Proper Sportsmanship
        1. Acknowledge opponent's good plays
        2. Otherwise, remain silent

   With an outline this good, writing a first-rate essay is a slam dunk.

BRAIN TICKLER
Set #37

With a presidential election coming up, your social studies teacher wants you to write a composition about "Your Favorite President in American History." Because you have recently studied the Civil War, you've had ample reason to admire the presidency of Abraham Lincoln. (Also, it's fresh in your mind.)

Write a brief outline that will help you write this essay. You may need to consult a source or two on Lincoln just to refresh your memory.

Now that you've mastered the arts of note-taking and outlining, you're ready for your next challenge: examinations.

BRAIN TICKLERS
THE ANSWERS

Set #33, page 116

Answers will vary, but a graphic organizer could look like this:

Similarities	Differences
• Each stanza is four lines long	• In 1st stanza, narrator is "in love"; in 2nd stanza, "fancy passes by"
• Each stanza has a similar rhyme scheme (1st and 3rd lines rhyme; 2nd and 4th lines rhyme)	• In 1st stanza, people marvel how well-behaved narrator is; in 2nd stanza, everyone notices narrator is himself again
• Each stanza has same narrator and "you"	

Set #34, page 118

Answers will vary, but a good outline could resemble this one:

The Plot of "The Monkey's Paw"
  I. Conflicts
    A. Internal
      1. Mr. White's desire for adventure vs. danger of the paw
      2. Mr. White's guilt (re: son's death) vs. danger of the paw
    B. External: Mr. White vs. Mrs. White (re: the second wish)
  II. Crisis: Mr. White's 3rd wish
    A. Prevails over Mrs. White
    B. Eliminates power of the paw
  III. Resolution: results of the crisis
    A. Reconciliation with Mrs. White
    B. Dealing with grief over the loss of their son

Set #35, page 122

Answers will vary, according to the text you consult and your reading of it. However, your outline could look like this one:

  C. America Remains Neutral
    1. President Wilson's policy of isolation (not getting involved)
      a. Tries to involve Allies/Central Powers in peace talks
      b. Favors stronger military "just in case"
    2. Americans are divided
      a. Most favor allies
      b. Some favor Central Powers
        (1) Those of German/Austrian ancestry
        (2) Irish-Americans oppose England
        (3) Jewish-Americans favor Germany

      3. Effects of America's neutrality

         a. Economic boom—both sides (especially Allies) need resources from U.S.

            (1) Food

            (2) Weapons

         b. Propaganda spread by both sides in attempt to seek American sympathy

Set #36, page 127

Roy Campanella's spirit and leadership were evident in his exploits on and off the baseball field. A catcher for the Brooklyn Dodgers, Campanella won the National League's Most Valuable Player Award three times and led the Dodgers to their first World Championship in 1955. Campanella was one of the first African-Americans to break baseball's color barrier. His career ended prematurely after the 1957 season when, as the result of an automobile accident, he became paralyzed from the chest down. Campy worked very hard to regain partial use of his arms and hands.

Outline answers will vary.

    Roy Campanella: Spirit and Leadership
       I.   Pre–Major League Baseball
      II.   Campy's Career with the Dodgers
     III.   The Accident & Life after Baseball

Set #37, page 130

Answers will vary, but this outline includes some of the more important aspects of Lincoln's life and presidency.

Abraham Lincoln: My Favorite President
   I. Overcame personal challenges
     A. Difficult childhood
       1. Poverty
       2. Death of his beloved mother
       3. Very little formal education

    B. Political challenges

       1. Lost Illinois Senate election to Douglas

       2. Came from nowhere to win presidency over favorites in both parties

II. Presidential accomplishments

    A. The Civil War

       1. Would not compromise on freedom for African-American slaves

       2. Believed in maintaining the nation at all costs

       3. At war's end, determined to heal wounds

    B. Lincoln's "style"

       1. Marvelous writer and speaker

          a. Gettysburg Address

          b. 2nd Inaugural Address

       2. Worked especially well with his rivals

          a. Selected best people available

          b. Did not take criticism personally

          c. Welcomed opinions that differed from his

CHAPTER SIX

How to Study for Tests and Quizzes (and How to Ace Them)

"Oh, no! We have a science test on Friday!"

You know that multiple factors produce the grades that you receive on your report cards. You will be graded on your classwork, homework, class participation, group work, essays, papers, projects, speeches, performances, portfolios, lab work, journals, and other factors that depend upon the idiosyncrasies of your different teachers.

Despite these many different endeavors, you understand that the two most important factors will probably be tests and quizzes.

What's the difference between a test and a quiz? To put it simply, a quiz is like a mini-test. It is based on a smaller chunk of material: it is likely to evaluate a smaller number of skills, concepts, and facts. A quiz will usually take less than a full period, whereas a test may keep you working right up until the bell rings. Chances are you will have less notice of an upcoming quiz and therefore less time to prepare. Finally, a quiz counts less. (Some teachers even add up a number of quizzes and count them as a single test.)

That said, two fundamental similarities outweigh these differences. For one thing, your teachers give tests and quizzes because they want to find out how well you are learning what they are teaching. A second major similarity: both may generate considerable anxiety.

There are two kinds of test anxiety. One is unproductive, and one is helpful. There's the overwhelming, "Oh-no-I'll-never-pass-this-test!" anxiety that keeps you from preparing properly and leaves you unprepared and overwhelmed when you actually sit down to take the test. That kind of anxiety is obviously unproductive. The other kind can help you. It's the anxiety that comes, on the one hand, with knowing that you have prepared well and, on the other, with realizing that the admittedly important test you are about to take will challenge your best preparation. It's what a first-rate quarterback like Peyton Manning probably feels when he lines up opposite a formidable defense: he knows this defense will require his best performance.

The point is this: you may always experience test anxiety—the best students do—but this chapter will prepare you for the second kind.

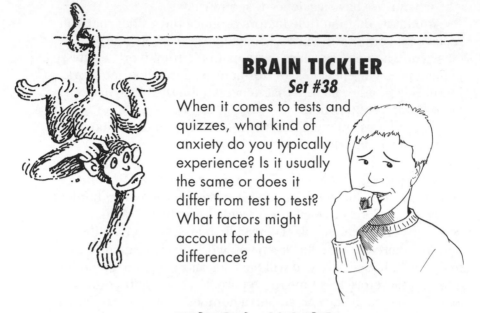

BRAIN TICKLER
Set #38

When it comes to tests and quizzes, what kind of anxiety do you typically experience? Is it usually the same or does it differ from test to test? What factors might account for the difference?

EVERY NIGHT: THE BEST APPROACH TO STUDYING

Check out this scenario, and see if it sounds familiar.

Your Spanish teacher announces on Monday that she's giving a test on Friday of the same week. She tells you exactly what will be on the test, and you copy this information from the board. On Thursday, when you stroll into Spanish class, you see written on the board in large letters, "TEST TOMORROW! STUDY!" These words you also copy into your planner.

That night, you dispose of your homework as quickly as you can because you know you're going to need significant time to prepare for this exam. You have a lot of vocabulary to learn, and you never really understood the featured verb tense, so you'll have to learn it tonight.

The work is as difficult as you anticipated, and it's taking even longer than you expected. With the second marking period drawing to a close, you know that your grade is hovering in that good ol' B-to-C range, so this test means a lot. This kind of pressure you don't need.

It's after 11:00. Your eyes feel hot and itchy. Your parents keep reminding you that it's time to get to bed, and your body is starting to agree with them. You wish you knew the Spanish material better. Maybe you can study a little more in homeroom. Maybe Señora will offer test corrections. Maybe there's some extra credit you can do.

Does this sound familiar? Well, that's one way to go about it, and you'll learn (if you don't know already) that some people take that approach to life in general. It could be high school and college students who have to pull "all-nighters" to study for a test or write a paper. It could be an employee who coasts until the proverbial eleventh hour and then has to put in tons of overtime to get the job done on time. It could be a grown-up who, before filing his income taxes, lets the April 15th deadline come and go and must then pay tax penalties. That's one approach, and for some people it lasts a lifetime.

There is, however, a better way.

And, to put it in its simplest terms, here it is: study every day. (OK, so maybe not *every* day, since, way back in Chapter 1, you agreed it would be a good idea to take one day off every week.) Reading those three words—"Study every night"—might send you into a state of near-cardiac arrest, but before you permit yourself to perish, just keep in mind these few advantages:

- Studying this way will actually save you time because you will need less time to learn the material. The more often you encounter a particular study fact, the quicker you will be able to commit it to memory.
- Studying this way will foster a sense of mastery, which will lead to greater confidence and better grades.
- Whether you're breaking or building habits, the beginning is the hardest part. But once you get past that, you begin to reap huge benefits. That's the thing about study habits: they get to be second-nature.

Are you convinced yet?

Well, let's move on. Now, a couple of pointers on studying and time management:

1. First, complete whatever is due tomorrow. Whatever that is— whether it's science homework or a reading journal or a sheet of math problems or verb conjugations— get it done first. Then set aside time to study.

2. Study more when homework is light. You know you don't get the same amount of homework every night; some nights you might get very little. Use that free time to get in some extra studying. It will make your life much easier later on.

3. The same goes for your other commitments. Study more when you have the free time. If you have a sixty-minute guitar lesson, you won't have as much time for studying. On the other hand, if it's a really slow Sunday, put in a couple of hours. Spread it out so it doesn't feel onerous.

4. The day before a test, you may want to study only the subject in which you'll be tested. Of course, if you really follow this method, you may not need that much time to review what you already know.

What to Study

Now that you have a grip on the question of *when* to study, you need to think about *what* to study. To accomplish this, you need to focus in two directions, backwards and forwards. In other words, on the one hand, you have to review what you've already learned. On the other, you need to think ahead and ask yourself what material you'll be required to know when your next exam comes around.

Let's examine the "already learned" part of it. This happens to be the easier part because basically it simply involves your reviewing your class notes for that day. You're going to revisit briefly the major events in each class. This shouldn't take that long. First of all, you were just there a few hours ago, so most of the material will be fresh in your mind. Second, there's a very good possibility that, in doing your homework, you already revisited these major events. For example, your math homework probably required you to practice the exact mathematical concepts and operations that you learned in class. If that day's class taught you how to compute the slope of a straight line, it stands to reason that your homework will revisit that territory.

But the review of some subjects might not be so automatic. That would depend, of course, upon whether you experience any difficulty with the material you encounter.

Let's say your English teacher had been working on pronoun-antecedent agreement. *Pronoun-antecedent agreement*? What does that even mean? You didn't quite get it in class, and examining the material in the comfort of your bedroom doesn't seem to make that much of a difference. Obviously, this kind of material will require additional time and attention.

Or what if your social studies class focused on the problems emerging from America's effort to reconstruct the Union after the Civil War? As you review your notes from that day's lesson, you come across an outline that looks, in part, like this:

I. First phase of Reconstruction: Returning Southern states to Union

    A. President Lincoln's Ten Percent Plan favors quick return

        1. Southern states readmitted to union when:

            a. 10% of voters swear oath of Allegiance to U.S.

            b. 10% of voters agree to follow emancipation

        2. States then establish new gov'ts.

        3. May create new constitutions, which must abolish slavery

    B. Opposition to Lincoln's plan

        1. Radical Republicans want to punish South and don't believe in South's willingness to change

        2. Radical Republicans take control of Army to

            a. Enforce vote for black males

            b. Prevent many white Confederate leaders from voting

        3. Scalawags (Southern white Republicans) and carpetbaggers (Northern reformers) come to power

        4. Redeemers (Southern Democrats) charge corruption and oust Republicans by 1877

Let's face it: you can't just skim an outline as dense with information as this one is. You have to read it and think about it until it makes sense and you can trace the relationship between cause and effect. If the material you encounter is routine, you will need less time. If it is challenging and complex, you will need more.

So that's part one of your studying—a quick review of the day's material. What about part two, getting ready for your next exam? Let's say that by Monday you know that on Friday of that week you will be taking a math test on ratios, rates, and proportions, a topic that your class has been studying for a few weeks. How do you go about getting ready for this test?

Well, the first thing you have to do is get yourself organized. In order to ready yourself for that exam, you will need to have your notebook and your textbook. But, first, some questions about the former.

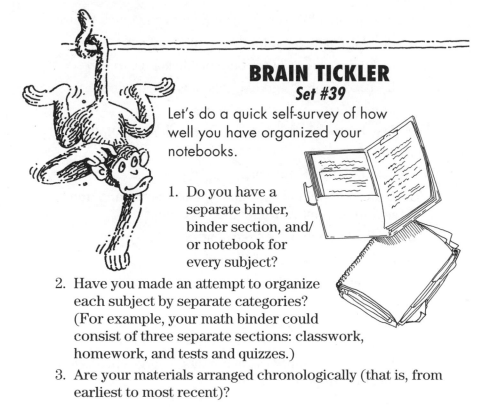

BRAIN TICKLER
Set #39

Let's do a quick self-survey of how well you have organized your notebooks.

1. Do you have a separate binder, binder section, and/ or notebook for every subject?

2. Have you made an attempt to organize each subject by separate categories? (For example, your math binder could consist of three separate sections: classwork, homework, and tests and quizzes.)

3. Are your materials arranged chronologically (that is, from earliest to most recent)?

4. Have you made an effort to find a proper place for all your loose papers?

5. Do you clean out your notebook/binder periodically (say, at the end of each unit or each marking period)?

6. Do you take your notebooks/binders home with you every day?

If you have organized your materials properly, you will have a much easier time with your nightly studying. For one thing, you won't have to waste valuable time looking for things. For another, the organization of your materials will make sense, you will be able to proceed in an orderly manner, and you will be able to learn more easily.

Let's get back to ratios, rates, and proportions. Assuming that this is not your first math test of the year, you should have a pretty good sense of how your teacher goes about preparing you for exams. In other words, for which material are you responsible? If you focus only on your class notes and handouts, will you be OK? Does your teacher tell you that it would be wise to review your homework? To what extent are you responsible for the chapter in the textbook? A good teacher will be very clear and very consistent about these concerns. In any case, these are questions that you must answer.

Next, you must decide on your approach to studying. You know that you have four nights to get ready, so what strategy will work best for you? Maybe you will use Monday night for ratios, Tuesday night for rates, and Wednesday for proportions. Then you can spend Thursday reviewing the whole shebang. Or maybe you know that you have ratios down pat and that you only have to focus on rates and proportions. Regardless, make sure you decide upon a plan.

This brings you to perhaps the most important step. You know *when* you're going to study, you know *what* you're going to study, and you even have all the materials you'll need. Your next concern is simply *how* to study.

MEMORIZATION AND CONCEPTUAL LEARNING

Consider these three situations:

1. Your class has been reading Charles Dickens's novel *Great Expectations*. In order for you to understand this difficult book, your teacher has given you an extensive vocabulary list. Now you have been told that you will be quizzed on the first fifty words on the list.

2. Your science class has been working on a unit on electricity and magnetism. For an upcoming test, your teacher has told you that you will be asked to explain in writing why your house is wired in a parallel, and not a series, circuit.

3. Your French teacher has been teaching you the difference between two verb tenses, the *passé compose* and the *imparfait*. On your next test, you must show that you know when to use each tense and how to conjugate familiar verbs in both tenses.

How do these tasks differ from each other? The first, a vocabulary quiz, is as close to pure memorization as you can get. The second, which involves understanding the difference between two kinds of circuits, is a mostly conceptual task. (Yes, you do need to *memorize* the definitions of the two, but in order to answer the question about your house's wiring, you mostly need to *understand* the difference.) The third task is the most complex. First of all, you need to understand that the passé compose is used to indicate that an action began and was completed in the past ("I attended kindergarten at the Woodrow Wilson School") and that the imparfait is used for actions that have begun in the past but continue in the present ("I have been a soccer fan for many years"). But on top of that, you also need to memorize the correct way to conjugate verbs in both tenses.

In the real world, situations requiring pure memorization or pure conceptual learning are very rare. Most of the time, you will be tested on both.

The important thing for you to accept is that almost always some memorization is required.

So what's the easiest, least painful way to memorize material?

Well, it sort of depends upon your learning style. Which one of the following applies to you?

- Are you a **visual** learner? Do you learn material best by seeing it?
- Are you an **auditory** learner? Do you learn material best by saying it and hearing it?
- Are you a **kinesthetic** learner? Do you learn material best through muscular movement?
- Are you a **tactile** learner? Do you learn material best through touching and feeling it?
- Do you learn best through some combination of the above ways?

Most of us (approximately 65 percent) are visual learners, so if you're not sure, that's probably a pretty good place to start. But you should experiment and see if you learn best through another sense.

What are the implications for this? Well, if you are an auditory learner, you will need to say things aloud. A kinesthetic learner might need to perform physical actions to learn material. A tactile learner might need to run his finger over words written in crayon.

Whatever works, go with it.

But regardless of learning style, there are a few basic memorization principles and methods that you should know:

- Write everything out by hand. It is easier to learn material written in your own hand. (Besides, writing the material for this purpose counts as a single kinesthetic repetition.)
- Using index cards, create flash cards, each containing a manageable chunk of information. If you're studying vocabulary for your French class, you might write the French word on one side and the English on the other. If you're studying the formula for the volume of a rectangular solid, you'd write "volume of rectangular solid" on one side and "$V = lwh$" on the other. If you're studying President Roosevelt's New Deal, you'd write "New Deal" on one side and a brief outline of key facts on the other. You get the picture.

- Repetition is essential to memorization. Begin by reading the cards. Then gradually, as you sense the material's increasing familiarity, begin to test yourself.
- Build on what you know. Memorization occurs in small chunks. If you need to memorize a poem, you might write the entire poem on one side of an index card, but you would not memorize the poem as a whole. You would read one line over and over until you learn it. Then you would add a second line. You would read both lines over and over until you've got them down pat. Then you'd move on to the next. If you were required to know the names of all sixteen teams in the National Football Conference, it would be easier for you to "chunk" the information. The NFC consists of four divisions, each with four teams. The Eastern Division, for example, contains the Dallas Cowboys, the New York Giants, the Philadelphia Eagles, and the Washington Redskins. Memorize that quartet first; then move on to another.
- Retention requires review. That's why one study session just won't get the job done. It is much better for you to memorize the material once and then reinforce that learning through review. (Of course, your later review sessions will go a lot faster than those initially spent on memorizing.)
- Focus. Promise yourself that you're going to master the material. If you're not "into it," if you've got other things on your mind, if you're going to permit lots of interruptions, well, then you're wasting your time.

Major Mistake Territory!

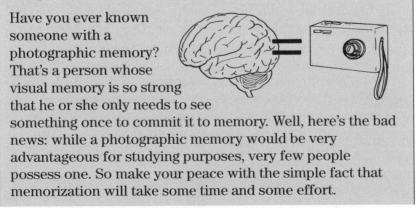

Have you ever known someone with a photographic memory? That's a person whose visual memory is so strong that he or she only needs to see something once to commit it to memory. Well, here's the bad news: while a photographic memory would be very advantageous for studying purposes, very few people possess one. So make your peace with the simple fact that memorization will take some time and some effort.

That time and effort will vary according to the subject. If you've been doing very well in Spanish and struggling in math, you should not be surprised if your study sessions for math require more time and greater focus.

Memory Aids

Did you ever hear of someone named Mnemosyne (Nuh-mah'-zuh-nee)? In Greek mythology, she was the goddess of memory (and the mother of the Muses). (Now that should give you some indication of how special the Greeks considered memory.) That's why various memory aids are called mnemonic (nuh-mah'-nik) devices or mnemonics.

Most mnemonics are based on taking the first letters of a series of objects and assigning a more easily memorable sequence of words to that series. This is a device known as an acrostic. Here are a few examples that you probably know:

- **Every Good Boy Does Fine** can help you remember the lines on the treble clef stave: E-G-B-D-F.
- **ROY G. BIV** can help you remember the colors of the spectrum: red, orange, yellow, green, blue, indigo, and violet.
- **HOMES** can help you remember the names of the Great Lakes: Huron, Ontario, Michigan, Erie, and Superior.
- **MY VERY EDUCATED MOTHER JUST SERVED US NINE PIZZAS** can help you remember the names and order of the planets of the Solar System: Mercury, Venus, Earth, Mars, Jupiter, Saturn, Uranus, Neptune, Pluto.

But acrostics are not the only kind of mnemonic. Here are a few simple sayings or rhymes that help us retain information:

- Spring ahead; fall back. (In spring, we turn the clocks ahead; in fall, we turn them back.)
- "I" before "E," except after "C," or when sounded like "A" as in "neighbor" or "weigh."
- Thirty days hath September, April, June, and November.

Sometimes even the look of a word will provide a helpful clue:

- "Stalactites" contains a "c," as in "ceiling."
- "Stalagmites" contains a "g," as in "ground."

As you can see, mnemonics can be helpful and amusing. Thinking of good ones can be time-consuming, so you might ask your teacher if he or she knows of any. Another good source is the Internet. Just use as your keyword "mnemonic" and see what you find.

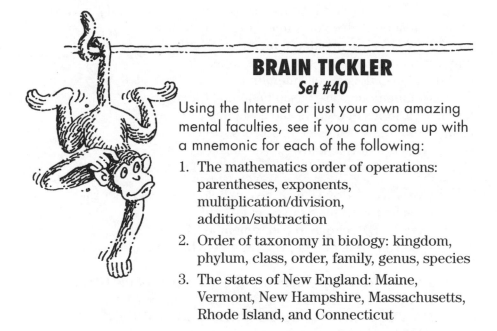

BRAIN TICKLER
Set #40

Using the Internet or just your own amazing mental faculties, see if you can come up with a mnemonic for each of the following:

1. The mathematics order of operations: parentheses, exponents, multiplication/division, addition/subtraction

2. Order of taxonomy in biology: kingdom, phylum, class, order, family, genus, species

3. The states of New England: Maine, Vermont, New Hampshire, Massachusetts, Rhode Island, and Connecticut

These kinds of memory aids may be fun to use, and they may save you some time, but you're going to get your best mileage out of the index/flash cards you create. This is where you will record most of the material you need to learn. This is where you will spend most of your study time. Therefore, it's essential that you create and use these cards properly.

Again, the guiding principle here is "chunking": You want to set up each card so that it has a sensible chunk of information. That could be a single definition or a mathematical formula or the difference between two scientific concepts, like *speed* and *velocity.* If you can use both sides of the card—one for the topic, one for the information—then do so. If you only need one side of the card, fine.

Sometimes you're going to have to learn an entire outline. It's really pretty easy to transform your outlines to index/flash cards. For example, take another look at the Reconstruction outline presented earlier in this paragraph. You might very well write on one side:

I. First phase of Reconstruction: Returning Southern states to Union

   A. President Lincoln's Ten Percent Plan favors quick return

Then on the other side of the card, you could record the details of Lincoln's plan:

   1. Southern states readmitted to union when

      a. 10% of voters swear oath of Allegiance to U.S.

      b. 10% of voters agree to follow emancipation

   2. States then establish new gov'ts.

   3. May create new constitutions, which must abolish slavery

BRAIN TICKLER
Set #41

Chapter 5 presented an outline on Guy de Maupassant's use of irony in "The Necklace." How would you create index/flash cards for that outline? How many cards would you create? Where would you record the information?

Once you've created the cards, you need to memorize their contents. Employ the principles discussed earlier. Repeat the process of reading each card until it begins to feel familiar. Gradually begin to test yourself: Look at one side of the card, and see if you can correctly recite the other. Review. Remember that you will learn the material more efficiently if you study over several days.

This brings you to the last step of studying, but, depending upon the nature of the exam, it could very well be the most important. It's called *practicing*.

There's a very good chance that your math tests and at least major parts of your science tests will consist of problems that you need to solve. These problems, usually complex in nature, test whether you can successfully apply the facts and concepts that you have learned. Solving them may depend to some degree on memorization, but they go beyond that.

Let's say that your math class has been working on proportions. On the upcoming test, you are likely to see word problems that look like the one you did in class:

You paid $13.50 at a nearby gas station for four gallons of gasoline. You know that you need 12.5 gallons to fill an empty tank. How much would you have to pay at that same gas station to fill that empty tank?

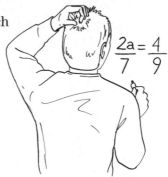

$$\frac{2a}{7} = \frac{4}{9}$$

$$\frac{4}{13.5} = \frac{12.5}{x}$$

$$\frac{4x}{4} = \frac{168.75}{4}$$

$$x = 42.1875 => \$42.19$$

You solved the problem correctly in class. How would you go about studying for the test?

The best way is to practice solving similar problems. Go through your class notes, go through the worksheets your teacher gave you, go through your homework, and go through the textbook. Undoubtedly you will find lots of problems that you can practice solving. And don't stop until you've achieved mastery.

BRAIN TICKLER
Set #42

You learn on Monday that your science teacher will be giving a test on Friday. The test will cover the work you have done on electricity and magnetism. The exam will cover electrical charges, electric currents, magnetism, and electromagnetism. You will be responsible for material discussed in class, the chapter in the textbook, related homework, and related labs.

Organize your study schedule for four nights.

PREPARING FOR AN ESSAY EXAM

In certain subjects, like English or social studies, you will find yourself preparing for exams that consist partly or completely of essays. Of course, if your teacher gives you the question ahead of time, you can prepare very easily and efficiently. However, even if you don't have the question, you can do a good job of anticipating what the question will be.

If your teacher gives you the essay question, he or she will probably put some limits on what kinds of preparation are considered acceptable. For example, your teachers will almost certainly not permit you to pre-write the essay at home. In most cases, you will be told that you may prepare an outline or a graphic organizer, and that is exactly what you will do. There is some chance that your teacher may tell you that you may not bring with you any materials at all. In that case, you may prepare the outline and, using your superb study skills, commit it to memory.

If you do not know the question beforehand, you can still prepare effectively, but you will need to take a few extra steps:

1. Ask your teacher for some additional information. Tell your teacher that you would like to prepare for the exam and that a list of potential topics would be helpful. Perhaps your teacher will comply.

2. Review your class notes, worksheets, and homework. Look for certain themes that the teacher has emphasized throughout the unit. (For example, a class studying Charles Dickens's *Great Expectations* would have repeatedly discussed the author's references to guilt and punishment.) Take a close look at certain lessons that easily could be converted to essay questions. (For example, an aim such as "How does Guy de Maupassant create an effective surprise ending?" could easily become an essay question.)

3. Review the essays this teacher has previously given. Perhaps your social studies teacher has demonstrated a fondness for compare-and-contrast essay questions. You can use this tendency to prepare for your current exam. Maybe you will be asked to compare and contrast the attitudes toward Reconstruction of President Lincoln and the Radical Republicans?

(Chapter 7 will provide some detailed information about writing superior essays.)

A TEAM EFFORT: STUDYING WITH FRIENDS

Later on, when you get to college, graduate school, or professional school, you will find that study groups are practically a necessity of academic life. Professors encourage students to form them, and many students simply wouldn't know what to do without them. There's a good reason for that, too: professors know that in the "real world," the world of work, things get done because people work well together.

Even on the secondary level, studying with friends is a great idea for lots of reasons. The main one is that two heads (or more) are better than one. When you study with friends, you can each benefit from the input of others. Someone will be able to explain a concept with which another student struggles. Someone else will remember some material that the rest of the group has overlooked. A third someone will be able to anticipate a question that may appear on the test.

There are other reasons, too. Working with a peer group can get your competitive juices flowing, providing additional incentive for you to learn the material well. At the very least, the time spent with your study group is time spent, well, studying, and that's good. And of course studying with friends can take the pain out of studying.

Before you gather with friends to prepare for a test, it's essential that you consider some very important matters:

- Choose your group carefully. You want to study with friends who are as serious and dependable as you are. The friends you study with might not be the same ones you'd call for the latest gossip. And remember that you're doing this because you, too, want to get something out of it. You don't want to be the only study group member who's done the work.
- Establish the particulars in advance. Where will you meet? When will you meet, and how long will you work? What should everybody bring? Exchange phone numbers beforehand.
- Keep the focus. Begin punctually. At the beginning of the session, create a schedule that includes topics, breaks, meals, and review. If the group's attention begins to wander, gently refocus. Decide together that you will not permit interruptions. That means that everyone turns off his or her cell phone!

Above all, as you review the material, decide how you can help each other. Is your time best spent discussing the conflicts in the novel you are studying? Would it be better if you quizzed each other on the vocabulary words you need to know? Should you spend some time working through practice problems similar to those you expect to find on the test?

How do you know if you've had a good study session? By the time the session ends, you should feel as if you've helped and been helped. You should feel that you've covered a lot of ground. You should feel that you've reduced the time you need to study alone.

Major Mistake Territory!

Let's face it. You elect to study with your friends because it's fun. If you're gathering to prepare for a science test, you're not going to spend four hours talking only about your unit on electricity and magnetism. These are you friends, and you're going to want to talk about some of the things that always find their way into your conversations.

But that's not why you're here! So you need to keep it to a minimum, and you need to choose study group friends who can do that. You know the expression, "It doesn't take too many rotten apples to spoil the barrel." That's certainly the case with study groups. Even one difficult group member— someone who's late or unprepared or hyper or unfocused— can ruin the group dynamic, and the work won't get done.

If that happens to your study group, you need to think about whether you want that individual to return . . . or whether you want to return to the group yourself. Studying takes a lot of time and effort, too much to waste.

IF YOU JUST DON'T GET IT . . . .

Your math teacher announces an upcoming test on graphic linear equations. Your first reaction: "Oh, no!" This is a moment you've been dreading because this whole linear equation business is simply Greek to you. What can you do?

Sources are available to you, help is on the way, but you need to act in a timely fashion. You need to act proactively. If you wait until the last minute, you may discover that the world does not always bend to your will, and the sources you had expected to be available are not.

So the best time to do something about linear equations is a.s.a.p.—as soon as possible—right after the teacher introduces the material and you don't get it.

To whom can you turn? What's your very best move? Here are a few, ranked in order of preference:

1. Go directly to your teacher. Whether it's called "Extra Help" or "Office Hours," teachers set aside time to work with students individually or in small groups. These sessions occur before school, during lunch, and/or after school. In most cases, teachers cannot require students to attend; students must themselves decide to take advantage of this terrific opportunity. Teachers understand that some students won't get it all via full-class instruction, and they are only too happy to work with students who are motivated to relinquish free time in order to learn the material. It's a good idea, however, to check with your teacher beforehand. If you decide to come during lunch, you'll probably need a pass.

2. Go to a peer tutor. Many schools have formal peer tutoring programs in which excellent students provide assistance to their peers. These students could be in your grade or in a higher grade. Sometimes, high school students agree to work with middle school students. To find out more about this service, see your teacher or your guidance counselor.

3. Go to a friend or family member. People who care about you will be willing to give their time and expertise to help you. If you're lucky enough to have a sibling who's a year or two older, this material will probably be relatively fresh in his or her mind.

4. Go to an online help center. The Internet abounds with homework and study help centers. In fact, your school or school district may sponsor one. Often, these help centers are staffed by certified teachers who can help you with your study needs. Just type "math help," for example, into your search engine, and you'll be supplied with plenty of options.

5. Go to a professional tutor. A professional tutor will meet you at your home (or at some other mutually convenient location) at a convenient time and assist you with your studying needs. The downside? Professional tutors can be very expensive.

Major Mistake Territory!

Should you ask your parents for studying help? That could be a delicate situation. Your parents might be academic whizzes, and they might be more than willing to assist, but still you need to be cautious.

For one thing, your parents haven't studied this material in many years. Their knowledge of the material could be a little rusty. Furthermore, the way they learned it could be very different from the way you've been taught. For example, today's math students routinely use calculators to solve problems, but to students of a previous generation this could feel like cheating.

Second, since teenagers and their parents sometimes fail to see things "eye to eye," you probably don't want to add yet another source of conflict. Will your parent be curious as to why you didn't learn this in class? Will your parent second-guess your decision not to go to extra help? Will you grow frustrated if the session doesn't go smoothly?

Proceed with caution.

TAKING THE TEST

"I'm just not a good test-taker."

Have you ever heard someone utter these words? Have you ever expressed them yourself? What exactly does that mean, anyway?

The truth of the matter is this: what matters most is the many hours that precede the single forty-minute period during which the test is taken. If you've paid attention, if you've done the work in and out of school, if you've studied conscientiously, you're going to do well on your tests.

That said, there are some strategies that will enhance your performance in a test situation.

First and foremost is time management. You may be acquainted with that awful moment when you realize that you must write an essay in the five minutes that remain in a test period. That's a situation you need to avoid. Here's what you need to do:

- As obvious as it may seem, make sure you can use the entire period for the test. In other words, visit the bathroom or get a drink of water before class. Make sure you come to class with whatever you'll need so that you don't have to run to your locker once the test gets underway.
- As soon as you get your test paper, give it a quick look so that you can determine the scope of the task that awaits you. Once you see that you have, for example, a brief matching section, a somewhat longer multiple-choice section, and three open-ended questions, each requiring a paragraph response, you can decide how much time you will allot to each. (Sometimes your teacher will offer suggestions about time management, which will make your task easier.) In your plan, always leave five minutes at the end so that you can check your answers.
- Don't spend too much time on questions you don't know. This is especially so if you're pondering a short-answer question that is worth one or two points.
- Check the time periodically. Your teacher may do you the favor of writing this information on the board.

A second concern is this one: "Oh, no, I don't know the answer!" Well, don't panic. That will only waste time and energy. The proper response depends upon the situation:

- Multiple-choice questions. You've read the question carefully, you've ruled out two obviously incorrect choices, but you can't choose between the remaining two. Look carefully at the remaining choices. Try to find a textual clue or a word such as "always" or "never" that would make one choice likelier than the other. If you cannot, venture a guess, anyway. You've given it your best shot.

- The wild guess. You've read the question, you've perused the choices, and you have no idea. Hey, it happens to the best of us. Just guess. Most tests do not penalize for incorrect answers. If you leave a question blank, it will certainly be wrong. If you guess—even wildly—you have some chance of getting lucky.
- The extended response (paragraph or essay). You've read the question, and you're just not sure if you can nail it. You've learned the material, but you just aren't certain if what you know fits this particular question. Again, give it your best shot. Remember to write good topic sentences that address the question directly. Remember to use ample details to support your ideas. (Chapter 7 will discuss this more fully.)

USING TEST RESULTS FOR SELF-IMPROVEMENT

When your teacher announces that he or she is returning test papers, you can only wait and pray. You note the expressions on the faces of your classmates and wonder if their glee or dismay is indicative of a trend that will include you.

If your grade is a good one, you feel pretty good about yourself, and you should. You worked well in and out of class, you learned the material, and you stepped up on test day.

If your grade is less than what you have expected, you will surely feel disappointed. But, whether your result was good or bad, you need to take stock of what worked or didn't work. Here are some questions you need to ask yourself:

- Was my performance on this test the result of previous gaps in knowledge? In most of your subjects, you build on what you already know. But what if there are gaps in your foundation? In math, for example, if you don't know the order of operations, you're not going to have an easy time with complex equations. If you haven't acquired the necessary building blocks, it's going to be hard for you to excel, no matter how hard you study the current material. It's important, however, that you recognize this deficiency and take steps to address it. Your first step should be discussing it with your teacher.

- Did you prepare effectively for this exam? Consider all the elements of academic success that this book has addressed. They involve making the most of your time and resources both in and out of school. For example, this chapter suggests that you develop a habit of nightly studying, instead of last-minute cramming. Have you done that? Earlier chapters address matters as different as sleep patterns and classroom behavior. Have you followed the book's advice? In any case, you need to take a good, hard look at what you've done and what you might do to improve.

- Should I discuss my results with my teacher? If your goal in doing so is to beg for a couple of extra points that you know you don't deserve, then no. But there are good reasons to go ahead and see your teacher. (First of all, extend to your teacher the courtesy of asking him or her when you might get together to talk about the test.) As you know, some degree of subjectivity often goes into the grading process, and it would not be unreasonable to ask your teacher to reconsider the way your paper was graded. Teachers grade many papers, and even though we would like to think they give 100 percent of their best attention to every one, that's probably unrealistic. At the very least, you can get an explanation of where you missed the mark. Most important, though, you should express to your teacher your desire to succeed in his or her class and ask his or her advice on how to do so.

Receiving test results gives students an excellent opportunity to develop a sense of humility. If you've done well on this exam, don't permit yourself to become overly confident. Remember that hard work made this success possible, and remain determined to develop superior work habits. And if you didn't do as well as you would have liked, consider the old saying, "Rome was not built in a single day." Remember that success takes time, and enjoy the satisfaction of small improvements.

BRAIN TICKLERS
THE ANSWERS

Set #38, page 138

Answers will vary. Some factors that might account for differences would be

1. How well you have prepared for a test
2. How well you have been doing in the class
3. How strong you are in this particular subject
4. How much you enjoy the subject
5. How much you like the teacher
6. How important the test is
7. How well you are managing your time
8. Other stress factors in your life

Set #39, page 142

Answers will vary, according to the requirements of each subject and each subject's teacher. A good rule of thumb: for each question, a "yes" is better than a "no"! Essential points are discussed within the text.

Set #40, page 148

Your answers will vary, depending upon your sources or your own ingenuity. These are acceptable:

1. Please excuse my dull, annoying sister.
2. Kids prefer cars over family, girls, and sports.
3. My very nice mother reads comics.

Set #41, page 149

Card 1, Side 1:

Why the Ending of "The Necklace" Succeeds

    I. Foreshadowing sets up surprise ending

Side 2:

    A. Mme. Forestier lends Mathilde "expensive" necklace

    B. Jeweler provided casket only

Card 2, Side 1:

Why the Ending of "The Necklace" Succeeds

  II. Small ironies prepare reader for bigger irony

Side 2:

    A. Mme. Forestier owns a fake necklace

      1. A rich person expected to own real diamonds

      2. Mme. F: a fake herself?

    B. Mathilde's sensational first night at the party is also her last night as a social success

      1. She is the hit of the ball

      2. Repaying their debts, she has neither time, money, nor beauty for partying

    C. With great pride Mathilde tells Mme. Forestier how she replaced the necklace

Card 3, Side 1:

Why the Ending of "The Necklace" Succeeds

  III. Point of view preserves element of surprise

Side 2:

    A. Third person limited omniscient—only through Mathilde's eyes

    B. Reader never learns what others (especially Mme. Forestier) are thinking

Set #42, page 151

Answers will vary.

Prior to your first night of study, you should have outlined your textbook reading.

Night one (Monday): Get yourself organized. Assemble your study materials by gathering your class notes, textbook outlines, homework assignments, and lab reports. Separate study materials into four categories: electrical charges, electric currents, magnetism, and electromagnetism. Create index/flash cards for study.

Night two (Tuesday): Study index/flash cards for the electric charges and electric currents.

Night three (Wednesday): Review index/flash cards for the electric charges and electric currents. Study index/flash cards for magnetism and electromagnetism.

Night four (Thursday): Review index/flash cards for entire unit.

Becoming a Better Writer

A number of years ago, "writing across the curriculum" became the latest trend in education. Suddenly, teachers in subjects as diverse as foreign language, science, and physical education began to sneak into their course requirements paragraphs, essays, and even research papers. The result was that students were writing more; since they were writing more, the reasoning went, they were writing better.

There's some validity to that way of thinking. If developing good study habits can improve grades, then developing a "writing habit" can lead to better writing skills. But the quantity of writing opportunities that come your way will not auto-matically result in qualitative improvement.

First, you need to work on developing specific skills. Having done so, then you need to practice them.

Let's begin by taking a look at the writing that you actually do.

Your first reaction might be to say, "Well, school aside, I don't actually write that much." But a closer look might produce a different conclusion.

BRAIN TICKLER
Set #43

Complete the chart below. Estimate the number of minutes you spend on each task. Base your responses on a typical school day. Don't worry: there's no right or wrong response!

Activity	Number of Minutes
At home	
• Writing messages	
• Compiling lists	
• Writing emails	
• Writing instant messages	
• Completing homework (writing only)	
At school	
• Taking notes in class	
• Completing class activities	
• Completing formal writing tasks (e.g., essays)	
• Taking tests/quizzes with a writing component	

The number of minutes you spend writing may fluctuate from week to week or year to year, but one thing is for certain: the longer your academic career, the more time you will spend with pen in hand (or keyboard below hands).

THE RIGHT WORDS

If you pick up the daily newspaper or watch the evening news report on television, you will come across an occasional language usage error. Professional journalists, whether in the print or broadcast media, make mistakes. The point: no one expects you to write flawlessly.

That said, you ought to be aware of what your teachers do expect of you. They expect you to develop a sense of mastery of the basics. They expect you to avoid errors that call unnecessary attention to themselves. They expect you to use the resources available to you.

Capitalization

You would think that capitalization would be a simple matter, but somehow it isn't.

The trick here is distinguishing between common nouns and proper nouns. A common noun is a general category of noun; a proper noun is a specific person, place, or thing. Consider the difference:

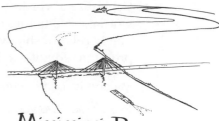

Mississippi River

> I live in a small town.
> I live in Smithtown.

Smithtown is the name of a specific town. Therefore, it is capitalized. This chart will show you how this principle applies to other kinds of nouns:

common river

Common Noun	Proper Noun
City, state	Baltimore, Maryland
Body of water	Atlantic Ocean, Mississippi River
Streets and highways	Lexington Avenue, Route 135
Nations	Poland, Republic of South Africa
Continents	Australia, Asia
Buildings	The Chrysler Building, Sears Tower
Schools	Parker Middle School, Duke University
Religions	Islam, Christianity
Nationalities, races	Italian, African-American
Languages	Mandarin, Spanish
Holidays	Passover, Fourth of July
Special events	Special Olympics, Tulsa Film Festival
Acronyms	NATO, UNICEF

That seems easy enough, but there are still some tricky situations with which you should be familiar:

- Capitalize a word showing a family relationship when that word is used before or instead of a person's name. If the family relationship word follows a possessive noun or pronoun, do not capitalize the word.

    My dad is a superb golfer. (*dad* follows the pronoun *my*)

    Jack asked, "Do you want to join me for a run, Dad?"
    (*Dad* is used instead of a person's name.)

- Do *not* capitalize the names of school subjects. Do capitalize a specific course or a language.

    My favorite subject is social studies.

    I am enrolled in Mr. McGowan's World History 101 class.

- Capitalize the title of a person if it comes before a name or if you are referring to a specific person in a high office.

    I would like to be a professor when I grow up.

    I look forward to Professor Wilson's class.
    (Title comes before a name.)

    Alice is the vice president of her company.

    The Vice President just called the Senate to order.
    (Title refers to a person in a high office.)

BRAIN TICKLER
Set #44

Ten sentences follow. If a sentence contains an error in capitalization, correct it.

1. My Mom earned a degree from Baruch College before starting work as an accountant.

2. Mr. Simmons, my science teacher, rarely gives homework on the weekends.

3. The East river separates Manhattan from Long Island.

4. Jerry was especially proud when his daughter received a promotion to vice president.

5. The Secretary of Defense announced that troops would soon be sent to this troubled region.

6. If you're interested in a unique experience, try spending new year's eve in Times Square.

7. Terry's latin teacher would not accept late homework.

8. I was hoping that Uncle Alex would join us for dinner.

9. I understand that a bunch of cool restaurants have opened on Smith street.

10. Professor Gibbons teaches lots of history courses, including American History 101.

Which Word(s) Should I Use?!

Some of the most conspicuous errors often turn out to be those habits that are hardest to break. In this category are those words that just might be spelled as one word or two.

Check out this chart, which should clear up some of the confusion:

The Problem	The Solution
a lot or *alot* or *allot?*	*a lot* means many *alot* is always wrong *allot* means the same as *distribute* or *assign*
each other or *eachother?*	There is no such word as *eachother*. Instead it is written as two words: *each other*.
everyday or *every day?*	*Everyday* is an adjective, which modifies a noun. In math, two hours of homework is an *everyday* event. *Every day* is an adverb. The soccer team practices *every day*.

This brings us to the next category: the dreaded homonym errors, words that sound the same but are spelled differently. For sure, these will be familiar to you.

The Problem	The Solution
to/too/two	to: a preposition—in the direction of We went to Yankee Stadium. too: also; a greater extent than desirable I am a Red Sox fan, too. I drank too much soda. two: the number I drank two cans of soda.
their/they're/there	their: personal pronoun showing ownership The Goodsteins love their dog, Molly. they're: contraction for they are They're joining us for dinner. there: in or at or to a place Sherry's school is right there.
here/hear	here: this place I go here for pizza every week. hear: to perceive sounds with the ear I hear too much chatting in this classroom.
it's/its	it's: a contraction for it is It's a beautiful day for a picnic. its: personal pronoun showing ownership The dog is searching for its bone.
your/you're	your: personal pronoun showing ownership I found your watch under the couch. you're: a contraction for you are I think you're a great friend.

who's/whose	who's: a contraction for *who is*
	Who's going to the party tonight?
	whose: personal pronoun showing ownership
	I wonder *whose* bag this is.

BRAIN TICKLER
Set #45

The following sentences may contain errors of the homonym or one word/two word variety. If the sentence contains an error, correct it.

1. My cousin likes to go for a swim everyday.

2. Every morning he wakes up and tells his wife, "Its a beautiful day for a swim."

3. He generally uses an outdoor pool, so in the winter months the water is just to cold.

4. Even at that hour, the pool can get kind of crowded, and the swimmers often bang into each other.

5. Sometimes they argue about who's lane is who's.

6. Often you might hear someone say, "Buddy, your in the wrong lane."

7. It's obvious that some people are very concerned about their health.

8. Either that, or they just love exercise allot.

9. My cousin once swam two miles, but I wasn't there to see it.

10. As my father always says, "They're are two kinds of people in this world, those who do and those who watch them do."

The Apostrophe

For a tiny drop of ink, the apostrophe causes way more than its share of trouble.

That's somewhat confusing, since the rules that govern its usage are mostly straightforward.

The first—and simpler—usage is the contraction. Here the apostrophe is used to indicate that a letter has been omitted when two words have been combined. Here are some familiar contractions involving pronouns and common verbs or helping verbs:

- I will see you later. => I'll see you later.
- You would do the same for me. => You'd do the same for me.
- He is a superb tennis player. => He's a superb tennis player.
- We have been to London before. => We've been to London before.

One common use of contractions involves combining a verb (or helping verb) and *not*. In this case, *not* is shortened to *n't* and added to the verb. Here are some examples:

- Terri has not attended band practice. => Terri hasn't attended band practice.
- Willie does not like soccer. => Willie doesn't like soccer.
- You should not start to smoke cigarettes. => You shouldn't start to smoke cigarettes.

You will come across these two exceptions to this rule:

- will not => won't
- cannot => can't

That's not all that complicated, right?

Using an apostrophe to make nouns possessive seems to get the better of many a secondary student.

Once again, the rules are straightforward:

- For a singular noun, add *'s*. (It doesn't matter if the word ends in *–s*.)

  Peter's dog is an uncommonly frisky creature.
  The Eiffel Tower is one of Paris's most familiar sights.

- For plural nouns ending in *–s*, add an apostrophe.

  The cities' mayors have assembled to discuss common problems.
  My parents' closest friends live in Michigan.

- For plural nouns that do not end in *–s*, add *'s*.

  The children's room needs a new coat of paint.
  The geese's feathers have fallen all over our lawn.

So the first question you need to ask yourself is this: is the possessive noun singular of plural? If it's singular, you just add *'s*. If the noun is plural, you need to determine whether it ends in *–s* (as most do) or in some other letter. If it ends in *–s*, simply add an apostrophe; if it ends in some other letter, add *'s*.

Major Mistake Territory!

Now that you know how to handle contractions and possessive nouns, you understand about 99.9 percent of the legitimate uses of apostrophes. The problem is that some students get stuck on *illegitimate* uses of apostrophes.

These fall into two main categories. You cannot use apostrophes in verbs or in possessive pronouns.

Each of these sentences contains an error of an almost unforgivable variety:

1. Jessica *want's* the whole world to know that she can sing beautifully.

   Wants is a verb. It does not have an apostrophe. Not ever.

2. Paul and Sadie hope that the house will soon be *their's*.

   Theirs is a pronoun. It does not have an apostrophe. Not ever.

Perhaps the confusion is the result of contractions involving verbs or pronouns. For example, it's OK to write *haven't* when you are combining *have* (a verb) and *not,* and it's OK to write *she's* when you are combining *she* (a pronoun) and *is.*

Whatever the source of the confusion, this is a mistake you must definitely avoid.

BRAIN TICKLER
Set #46

Some of these sentences contain errors involving apostrophes. Correct those mistakes.

1. The Syracuse University mens' team won the national championship.
2. Carmelo Anthony was the dominant player on that year's team.
3. As a pro, he's been voted to several all-star teams.
4. Spilt coffee has stained this books' cover.
5. Because of his illness, James lost three weeks' worth of salary.
6. Someone needs to pick up the children's toys.
7. I mistakenly took someone elses' hat.
8. I was wondering if this hat is your's.
9. Sally need's to get the assignments that she missed.
10. The ladie's clothing shop is located around the corner.

Miscellaneous Usage Problems

No, we're not quite finished. Remember that the purpose of this section is to help you to avoid the kinds of errors that will draw unwelcome attention. Well, these also fit into that category.

The Problem	The Solution
could of, would of, should of	All wrong! These errors likely result from the contractions *could've*, *would've*, and *should've*. Nevertheless, the correct combinations are *could have*, *would have*, and *should have*. I *should have* trained harder prior to the race.
have went	Wrong! The correct way to express this thought is by using the words *have gone*. I *have gone* three times to see this band in concert.
different than	Wrong! The correct expression is *different from*. The customs in this country are *different from* the customs in mine.
further/farther	*Farther* means a greater distance—an actual, measurable distance. She lives *farther* from the lake than I do. *Further* means to a greater extent; use with an "immeasurable" distance. His excuse couldn't be any *further* from the truth.
good and *bad* . . . and *well* and *badly*	*Good* is always an adjective; it modifies nouns and pronouns. *Well* is an adverb; it modifies verbs. This pizza is really *good*. (an adjective that modifies *pizza*) I played *well* at yesterday's game. (an adverb that modifies *played*)

	Bad is an adjective, and *badly* is an adverb. I am afraid I got a *bad* grade on the math test. (an adjective that modifies *grade*) I am afraid I performed *badly* on the lab test. (an adverb that modifies *performed*) Two related complications: a state of being verb usually gets the adjective form. Some of these verbs are: *to be, to seem, to appear, to look, to sound, to taste,* and *to smell.* You would not say, for example, that this pizza really tastes *well.* You would say that it tastes *good.* Also, if someone asks you how you are feeling, you may say, "I feel good," "I feel well," or "I'm not feeling well." However, you may not reply, "I feel badly."
between you and I	Incorrect! People think *"between you and I"* sounds proper, but it isn't. After *"between,"* you must use the object form of the pronoun. Can we keep this just *between you and me?*
someone (or *everyone* or *everybody*) and *their*	You cannot say that *everyone* must bring *their* book. *Everyone* is singular, but *their* is plural. *Everyone* must bring *his or her* book. *Someone* has forgotten to wear *his* jacket.

Major Mistake Territory!

Today's word processing programs contain very good spelling and grammar checks, most of which will alert you to errors as they occur. They are enormously helpful, and it would just be silly for you not to use them with your formal writing assignments.

These features are not fool-proof, however, and you cannot let them do all the editing. One reason is that they will not catch all your mistakes. For example, they will not catch many of the homonym killers listed earlier in this chapter. A second reason is that they might make corrections that you simply don't want. In other words, your computer could be wrong. That means that you need to know what is correct and what is not. You need to be the final authority on these matters.

BRAIN TICKLER
Set #47

Some of these sentences contain usage errors. Correct those mistakes.

1. Jackie pitched good, but the rest of the players made too many errors in the field.
2. I can run farther than Bill, but he can run faster.
3. Everybody has to study their notes because the test is going to be hard.
4. Terry could fight; he could of been a contender.
5. The doctor reported that the news was mostly good.
6. Between you and I, this newscaster needs a new wig.

7. American football is a lot different than the football most other nations play.

8. They could have went to Pretoria, but that would have taken another two days.

9. My first impression is that this song sounds really well.

10. The detective wanted to look farther into the witness's testimony.

SENTENCE SENSE

Now that you're well on your way toward reducing unwanted word errors, it's time to switch your focus to writing clear sentences.

Proper sentences convey whole units of meaning. When a group of words punctuated as a single sentence conveys either too little or too much information, problems result.

You are not reading a grammar text, but, in order to discuss this subject, the following terminology will be helpful:

- A **phrase** is a group of related words that contains neither a subject nor a predicate.
- A **clause** is a group of words that contains a subject and a predicate (or verb).
- An **independent clause** is a group of words that contains a subject and a predicate and expresses a complete thought. It can be punctuated as a sentence.
- A **subordinate clause** is a group of words that contains a subject and a predicate but does not express a complete thought. It cannot be punctuated as a sentence.

To the canvas. This is a phrase because it does not contain a subject or a predicate. *The talented painter slowly applied paint to the canvas.* This is an independent clause because it contains a subject (*painter*) and predicate (*applied*). It expresses a complete thought and is punctuated correctly as a sentence.

If you forget your book. This is a subordinate clause. It contains a subject (*you*) and a predicate (*forget*), but it does not express a complete thought and should not be punctuated as a sentence.

Consider this sentence:

I often visit the street where you live.

This sentence contains two clauses. The first, *I often visit the street*, is an independent clause. The second, *where you live*, is a subordinate clause. A sentence that contains an independent clause and a subordinate clause is called a complex sentence.

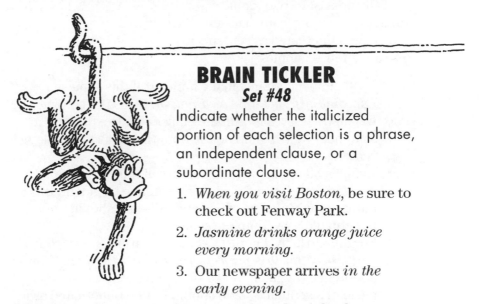

BRAIN TICKLER
Set #48

Indicate whether the italicized portion of each selection is a phrase, an independent clause, or a subordinate clause.

1. *When you visit Boston*, be sure to check out Fenway Park.

2. *Jasmine drinks orange juice every morning.*

3. Our newspaper arrives *in the early evening*.

4. My sister, *who lives in Oregon*, rarely makes it back to Florida.

5. *To apply for insurance*, you must be at least eighteen years of age.

6. *Because you are ill*, you really should skip the game.

7. *Who knows the time?*

8. *Running through the park*, I stumbled and nearly fell.

Now that you understand clauses, you are ready to diagnose two widespread sentence structure errors.

Sentence Fragments

A sentence fragment is just a piece of a sentence, incorrectly punctuated as if it were a complete sentence.

Sentence fragments generally consist of two kinds, phrases and subordinate clauses incorrectly punctuated as sentences. Here are a few examples:

- I will almost certainly make honor roll this semester. *Especially if I get an A in English.* (This is a sentence fragment. It is a subordinate clause—only a piece of a sentence—and should not be punctuated as a complete sentence.)
- Jamie is planning on going to Hawaii this spring. *To practice her surfing.* (This is a sentence fragment. It is a phrase—only a piece of a sentence—and should not be punctuated as a complete sentence.)
- For my birthday, I hope to get a new drill set. *Which I really need for this project I've been working on.* (This is a sentence fragment. It is a subordinate clause—only a piece of a sentence—and should not be punctuated as a complete sentence.)

How can you fix sentence fragment errors? It's easy! All you need to do is attach the fragment to a nearby independent clause. Let's fix the fragment errors above:

- I will almost certainly make honor roll this semester, especially if I get an A in English.
- Jamie is planning on going to Hawaii this spring to practice her surfing.
- For my birthday, I hope to get a new drill set, which I really need for this project I've been working on.

Major Mistake Territory!

This is a good time to consider the difference between formal writing and other, less formal forms of communication. If you are sending emails to or conducting a conversation with a friend, who cares if you employ sentence fragments?

How's it going?

Okay! You? Could be better. School again?

"What's up?"
"Not much. And you?"
"Going for a run."
"Where?"
"On the beach."
"Cool. Will you do your usual five-mile loop?"
"If I can."
You get the point, right?

(We've used some fragments in this book in order to maintain a "chatty" tone, but in formal writing [e.g. scholarly articles], sentence fragments aren't used.)

Run-on Sentences

While a sentence fragment is a piece of a sentence   in other words, not enough of a sentence to be punctuated as one—a run-on sentence contains too much information to be included in one sentence.

Quite simply, a run-on occurs when two independent clauses are incorrectly joined in a single sentence. Here's an example:

> The painter finished the room's walls and ceiling, then she moved on to the trim.

The problem here is that the first part of the sentence (*The painter finished the room's walls and ceiling*) is an independent clause. So is the second part (*then she moved on to the trim*). These cannot be joined with a comma. It's at that point that the sentence "runs on."

The hardest part of dealing with run-ons is diagnosing them in the first place. Once you've determined that a sentence runs on, it's relatively easy to fix. There are four basic ways to correct run-on errors:

1. Create two separate sentences. *The painter finished the room's walls and ceiling. Then she moved on to the trim.*

2. Use a semicolon to create a compound sentence. (A compound sentence is one that contains more than one independent clause.) *The painter finished the room's walls and ceiling; then she moved on to the trim.*

3. Use a coordinating conjunction to create a compound sentence. *The painter finished the room's walls and ceiling, and then she moved on to the trim.* The coordinating conjunction *and* joins the two independent clauses. Note: in a compound sentence, a comma always precedes the coordinating conjunction.

4. Use a subordinating conjunction to create a complex sentence. *After the painter finished the room's walls and ceiling, then she moved on to the trim.* The subordinating conjunction *after* changes the first independent clause to a subordinate clause.

These are the coordinating conjunctions you will most often use:

- and
- but
- or
- nor

- for
- so
- yet

The most common subordinating conjunctions are

after	because	since	when (whenever)
although	before	though	where (wherever)
as (as if, as though)	how	unless	whether
as long as (as soon as)	if	until	while

Be aware too that the relative pronouns *that, which, who, whom,* and *whose* may be used to introduce subordinate clauses. Here are a couple of examples:

- Sarah showed me the photos *that she had taken in Moscow.*
- Peter is the boy *who sits in the last seat.*

Major Mistake Territory!

There is a group of words and phrases that many writers incorrectly believe may be used to join independent clauses. Some of these are

- then
- however
- in fact
- nevertheless
- moreover

Consider the following run-on sentence:

> *Jerry Seinfeld's television show ruled the networks for nine years, the show won many awards for production and for ensemble and individual performances.*

Some students mistakenly believe that inserting one of the words listed above will correct the error. *Jerry Seinfeld's television show ruled the networks for nine years, in fact, the show won many awards for production and for ensemble and individual performances.* Inserting *in fact* does not correct the run-on. You would still need to add a semicolon: *Jerry Seinfeld's television show ruled the networks for nine years; in fact, the show won many awards for production and for ensemble and individual performances.*

BRAIN TICKLER
Set #49

The following paragraph contains several sentence fragment and run-on errors. Diagnose and correct these errors.

There's a lot to be said for living in a big city. Such as New York City. A city of this size offers very many cultural activities, a person would run out of money way sooner than he would run out of cultural choices. For example, take the theater. A theater-lover could attend Broadway, Off-Broadway, and Off-Off-Broadway productions. Not to mention the hundreds of plays produced in the outer boroughs. A skeptic could argue that the price of tickets is very high. To some extent that's true, however, a money-conscious customer can avail himself of half-price tickets at New York's famous TKTS's booth in Times Square. Also, while tickets to Broadway shows can run to more than $100, one could pay much less for other productions. The same applies to the huge number of this city's musical, dance, and operatic performances. If you're interested in that sort of thing. Furthermore, New York City has countless movie houses, many show several movies at once. And here's the great thing about New York: for absolutely no money at all, you can walk down Broadway or Madison Avenue or Fifth Avenue and enjoy the greatest people show in the world.

Keeping It Clear

You want your sentences to say what you mean, and eliminating sentence structure errors will certainly help you achieve that goal. But you're not quite out of the woods. Here are a few tips that will help you write clearer sentences:

1. Avoid excessively long sentences. An accomplished writer employs a mix of short, medium, and long sentences, but sometimes an overly long sentence, especially one joined by conjunctions, can be confusing for a reader. Do your reader a favor and turn an overly long sentence into two medium ones.

2. Avoid beginning too many sentences with *there is* or *there are*. It's a time-consuming construction. Avoid: *There are two foods I especially enjoy, pizza and ice cream.* Instead: *I especially enjoy two foods, pizza and ice cream.*

3. Use the active voice instead of the passive voice. The active voice refers to a sentence in which the subject acts. *Michael painted the garage.* The passive voice refers to a sentence in which something is done to the subject. *The garage was painted by Michael.*

4. Be careful about faulty comparisons. *Jenny loves me more than Peter.* This could mean that Jenny loves me more than she loves Peter or that Jenny loves me more than Peter does. This is easy to fix! When you make a comparison, be sure to use two verbs. *Leslie agrees with Rose more than she agrees with Stan.*

5. Make sure that your modifiers modify the words you want them to modify. Some of these errors can be amusing. *While drinking from his water bowl, Dad noticed that the dog seemed extra thirsty.* It sounds like someone should direct Dad to the sink, right? Well, this problem is called a dangling modifier: *drinking* modifies the subject of the nearby independent clause, *Dad.* Try either of these corrections: *While the dog was drinking from his water bowl, Dad noticed that he seemed extra thirsty* or *Dad noticed that the dog, drinking from his water bowl, seemed extra thirsty.* Here's another one: *I sold bags of candy to children with Cracker Jacks in them.* Again, this is easy to fix. Just move the modifier closer to the word it modifies. *I sold bags of candy with Cracker Jacks in them to children.*

BRAIN TICKLER
Set #50

Each of the following sentences contains an error that creates some confusion. Correct the error.

1. That church was designed by a world-famous architect.
2. Baked to absolute perfection, I served my homemade brownies.
3. Dana and Jeff visited the apartment on Warren Street that they had just bought.
4. There are many wonderful novels written by William Trevor.
5. Lenny likes rap more than Stephanie.
6. Because Terrence refused to fight, Brandon believed incorrectly that Terrence was a weakling and coward, and, when he spread around the school that this was so, even Terrence heard the rumor and decided to put Brandon in his place.

PARAGRAPHS

The ability to write a first-rate paragraph marks a critical point in a young writer's development. If you can produce a well-composed, informative, readable paragraph, you can then proceed without too much additional knowledge to write excellent essays and research papers. But the paragraph is basic. It's your opportunity to show that you can state your ideas and develop them in detail.

Teachers love writers who can write good paragraphs.

This chapter will now offer a recipe for producing such a paragraph. However, just as an accomplished chef may tinker with his ingredients, you will need to tailor this paragraph recipe to suit your own purposes.

Here is the recipe for a first-rate paragraph:

1. An opening sentence—a general statement of the topic

2. A topic sentence—an expression of the paragraph's main idea, specific to the question being discussed

3. Supporting details—the meat and potatoes of the paragraph, your chance to prove the point you've made in your topic sentence

4. A "clincher"—in effect, a second topic sentence, but a more authoritative one, because now you've proved your point

In order to apply this recipe to a real situation, let's take a look at the poem "Richard Cory" by Edwin Arlington Robinson:

Richard Cory

Whenever Richard Cory went down town,
We people on the pavement looked at him:
He was a gentleman from sole to crown,
Clean favored and imperially slim.

And he was always quietly arrayed,*   5
And he was always human when he talked;
But still he fluttered pulses when he said,
"Good morning," and he glittered when he walked.

And he was rich—yes, richer than a king—
And admirably schooled in every grace: 10
In fine,* we thought that he was everything
To make us wish that we were in his place.

So on we worked, and waited for the light,
And went without the meat, and cursed the bread;
And Richard Cory, one calm summer night,   15
Went home and put a bullet through his head.

    5. *presented; dressed*
    11. *in sum*

OK, so you've read the poem, the class has discussed it, and you understand fully the surprise ending of those last two lines. Now your teacher has given you this assignment for homework: write a paragraph about the poem's theme.

Using the recipe for a super paragraph, you might produce this piece of work:

> *It's not unusual for people to examine the lives of other people and maybe come away a little bit envious. That's what happens in Edwin Arlington Robinson's "Richard Cory," a poem that demonstrates once again that "the grass is sometimes greener on the other side of the hill." The narrator of this poem, a typical representative of the people of his town, admires and envies Richard Cory. Everything about Cory seems, well, perfect. He is well-groomed, well-mannered, well-educated, modest, and extremely wealthy. The narrator's use of expressions like "imperially slim" and "glittered when he walked" expresses the degree of admiration and prepares the reader for this statement of envy: "In fine, we thought that he was everything/ To make us wish that we were in his place." However, despite everyone's worship of him, Cory's life is very far from perfect. What causes his suicide? Could it have been loneliness? Maybe a broken heart? The narrator doesn't tell, and maybe he doesn't know. The point is that everyone's life contains its share of problems. The townspeople may have had to work hard to make ends meet, but the irony is that Cory probably would have gladly exchanged his problems for theirs.*

Consider the following points about this highly effective paragraph:

- Notice how the **opening sentence** begins to address the topic of the poem and the paragraph. It leads directly into the topic sentence without saying anything specific about the poem itself.
- Notice how the **topic sentence** includes key information about the work being discussed. It gives the title, the author, and the genre (poem). In addition, it clearly states the poem's theme, thus responding directly to the question.

- Notice how this paragraph is rich with **supporting details**. It identifies and explains the narrator and how he and his people feel toward Richard Cory. These two sentences—"The narrator's use of expressions like 'imperially slim' and 'glittered when he walked' expresses the degree of admiration and prepares the reader for this statement of envy: 'In fine, we thought that he was everything/ To make us wish that we were in his place.'"— support the assertion that Cory is admired and envied and lead into an effective discussion of the actual nature of Cory's life.
- "The point is that everyone's life contains its share of problems." This is a fine **clincher sentence**. Yes, it serves as a second topic sentence, but it carries so much more authority than the first. Why? Because the detailed discussion in the paragraph has already proved the writer's point.

This paragraph works very nicely because it contains all the necessary ingredients. It introduces an idea, states the idea, proves it with supporting details, and states it again for effect.

Using Quotes

Supporting details make all the difference. Your ability to make your case convincingly will go a long way in determining the grade you will receive. You can support your main point by providing one or more of the following:

1. Explanation
2. Discussion
3. Reasons
4. Facts
5. Examples

All are equally effective, as long as they are thoroughly developed.

One particular kind of detail that is especially effective is a quote. Why is a quote so effective? That's simple: you are using an original source, the author's own words.

However, using a quote is not that easy to do well. It takes practice. Here are some guiding principles you should keep in mind:

1. Use a quote when the author's words are especially convincing. In the "Richard Cory" paragraph above, using Robinson's words is practically required since the paragraph states that his word choices indicate the townspeople's envious feelings.

2. Don't use a quote without explaining what the author means. Some students think it's OK just to drop that quote in there and move on. It isn't. You need to explain how the author's words prove your point.

3. Don't use a quote and then paraphrase what the author has said. That's just redundant. You're saying the same thing twice.

4. Be careful about choosing an overly long quote. Your teacher is interested primarily in your ideas and in your ability to use the author's words to support your ideas.

5. Try to incorporate the author's words into the flow of your paragraph. Again, notice how the "Cory" paragraph accomplishes this.

6. Learn the rules for quoting within a paragraph. They are:

   a. If a quote is less than four lines and includes only one paragraph, simply include the quote within the text of your paragraph. Use quotation marks to indicate that you have used the author's words. This is what has been done in the "Cory" paragraph above.

   b. If a quote is four or more lines OR if a quote includes more than one paragraph, you must indent five spaces on both sides and single space the quoted material. You do not need to use quotation marks.

   c. Include page (or line) numbers in parentheses prior to your end punctuation.

   d. If you are quoting dialogue of less than four lines and of only one paragraph, use quotes within quotes.

Are you completely confused? Don't be. Your teacher will soon forgive a technical error of this nature and will instead admire your eagerness to use quoted material convincingly.

Major Mistake Territory!

Plagiarism is the academic equivalent of stealing. It is a very serious offense and could easily earn you a low grade.

Some students think that using an author's words is plagiarism, but it isn't. Plagiarism is using an author's words without *acknowledging that you have done so*. There's a huge difference.

Therefore, you need to keep in mind three simple things:

- Does the assignment give you the opportunity to use someone else's words? Sometimes your teacher will direct you to use a quote as a supporting detail, and sometimes your teacher will tell you that he or she is interested only in your words. Sometimes you may have to use your own judgment.
- Have you struck an effective balance between your own ideas and the words of another writer? Remember that your teacher probably wants to know what you know and expects to see another author's words only as supporting detail.
- Have you cited properly? In other words, have you used the methods listed above to make sure that you have given the author credit for his or her words?

Remembering these basic principles will serve you well as you advance in your educational life.

Shifting from One Idea to the Next

Sometimes writing can feel choppy because the author does a poor job of linking one idea to the next. If one idea or sentence ends and the next begins abruptly, the reader's reaction could be, "Huh?" That is a situation to be avoided.

To add fluidity and clarity to your writing, learn to make effective use of these transitional words and phrases:

The Writer's Purpose	Transitional Words and Phrases
To indicate a sequence	• then • first (second, third, etc.) • next • meanwhile • soon • later • eventually • finally
To provide an example	• for example • for instance • to illustrate
To explain cause and effect	• thus • therefore • consequently • for this reason
To add a similar idea	• in addition • similarly • likewise • moreover
To contradict an idea	• however • on the other hand • nevertheless • although
To explain importance	• primarily • in fact • especially • particularly

Keep in mind that these words can appear at the beginning or within a sentence. Furthermore, a word or phrase situated in one particular category could very well serve more than a single purpose.

BRAIN TICKLER
Set #51

Read the following poem, "Grass,"
by Carl Sandburg. In a good body
paragraph, answer this question:
Who is the speaker, and what is the
message of this poem? Use a quote
in your answer.

Grass

Pile the bodies high at Austerlitz and Waterloo.
Shovel them under and let me work—
    I am the grass; I cover all.

And pile them high at Gettysburg
And pile them high at Ypres and Verdun.   5
Shovel them under and let me work.
Two years, ten years, and passengers ask the conductor:
    What place is this?
    Where are we now?

    I am the grass.   10
    Let me work.

1. *Austerlitz and Waterloo were battles in which*
   Napoleon's armies fought.
5. *Ypres and Verdun were sites of battles in World War I.*

Writing Introductions and Conclusions

You know that an essay consists of three kinds of paragraphs: introductory, body (described above), and concluding. Introductions and conclusions can often stymie capable writers, but that needn't be the case.

An introduction consists of two groups of sentences, general and thesis. The general sentence(s) paraphrases the information presented in the question. The thesis sentence(s) expresses the essay's main idea. (If you are writing about literature, the thesis sentence will also provide the titles, authors, and genres of the works discussed.)

Let's say you encounter this question on an essay exam:

Everyone agrees that friendship is an essential part of growing up. However, nearly all friendships will at some point undergo some kind of trial, a test that the relationship must pass in order to continue.

From your readings this year, select two works in which friendships are tested. Identify the test that each must endure, and explain how and why the relationship is affected by this test. In your answer be sure to:

- *identify the test that the friendship must endure*
- *explain how the relationship is affected by this test*
- *explain why the relationship is affected this way*
- *use details from each work to support your ideas*

So how do you go about writing an introduction for this essay? It's easy. First, you want to create a general sentence, which means that you will be paraphrasing the information given to you. Well, what information is given to you? That's easy, too: just look at the first paragraph of the question. If you simply digest that information and produce your own version of it, you might come up with something like this:

Almost every friendship has to undergo a test. If the friendship survives that test, it will become stronger; if not, the friendship may perish.

Not bad, right? Next task: create a thesis statement. Remember that your thesis statement will express the essay's main idea, so it's very important that you get it just right. Here's an example:

In The Book Thief, *a novel by Markus Zusak, the friendship between Rudi and Liesel is tested by Germany's involvement in World War II. In Jane Austen's novel,* Emma, *the friendship between the main character,* Emma, *and Harriet is tested by Emma's meddlesome ways.*

If you put those two pieces together, you have a pretty good introductory paragraph.

Notice that each section of the introduction may contain more than one sentence. In this case, each contains two. Notice, too, how the introduction moves from a general statement to a more specific thesis statement. This movement from the general to the specific will be continued within the body of the essay.

If students find introductions befuddling, then the same can surely be said for conclusions. In fact, conclusions are even more mystifying because there really is no ready-made formula for writing them. A good conclusion is as unique as the essay it completes.

What should a good conclusion accomplish? It should bring the essay to a tidy end, it should leave the reader intellectually satisfied, and it should return the reader from the specificity of the body section to a general statement, thereby reversing much of the essay's momentum.

That may seem like a lot to accomplish, but it isn't. Here are a few steps to consider as you write conclusions:

- Re-read your essay. This is an essential step. Your essay is your work entirely. Only by fully understanding what you have created can you begin to be aware of how you will wrap it up.
- Re-state your essay's main idea. Paraphrase the ideas presented in your introduction. What a clincher sentence does for a paragraph, your conclusion does for your essay. The word *essay* comes from the French verb *essayer*, which means "to try." Well, most of your essay has tried to present and build a case. Now you have completed that attempt; therefore, your conclusion brings the added weight of authority.

- Bring your essay back to the general. Let's say you have written an essay about friendships in *The Book Thief* and *Emma*, as described above. What do those two books have in common? Well, each describes a friendship tested in some way. But, having written the essay's body, you realize that the ways are very different. Liesel's and Rudi's friendship is tested by a catastrophic world event. Emma's and Harriet's is tested by a flaw in Emma's character. That's excellent material for a conclusion. You can write about how wildly different the tests can be.
- Leave your reader on a high note. There's nothing worse than a conclusion that exists solely because an essay must end with one. Give yours the time and thought it deserves. A tight, insightful conclusion shows your reader that there's been no let-up of intellectual energy on your part.

BRAIN TICKLERS
THE ANSWERS

Set #43, page 165

Answers will vary.

Set #44, page 168

1. mom
2. correct
3. East River
4. correct
5. correct
6. New Year's Eve
7. Latin
8. correct
9. Smith Street
10. correct

Set #45, page 171

1. every day
2. It's
3. too
4. correct
5. whose ... whose
6. you're
7. correct
8. a lot
9. correct
10. there

Set #46, page 174

1. men's
2. correct
3. correct
4. book's
5. correct
6. correct
7. else's
8. yours
9. needs
10. ladies'

Set #47, page 177

1. well
2. correct
3. his or her
4. could have been
5. correct
6. Between you and me
7. different from
8. could have gone
9. good
10. further

Set #48, page 179

1. subordinate clause
2. independent clause
3. phrase
4. subordinate clause
5. phrase
6. subordinate clause
7. independent clause
8. phrase

Set #49, page 184

1. There's a lot to be said for living in a big city, such as New York City. (This corrects a sentence fragment error.)

2. Because a city of this size offers very many cultural activities, a person would run out of money way sooner than he would run out of cultural choices. (This corrects a run-on sentence error.)

3. A theater-lover could attend Broadway, Off-Broadway, and Off-Off-Broadway productions, not to mention the hundreds of plays produced in the outer boroughs. (This corrects a sentence fragment error.)

4. To some extent that's true; however, a money-conscious customer can avail himself of half-price tickets at New York's famous TKTS's booth in Times Square. (This corrects a run-on sentence error.)

5. The same applies to the huge number of this city's musical, dance, and operatic performances, if you're interested in that sort of thing. (This corrects a sentence fragment error.)

6. Furthermore, New York City has countless movie houses, and many show several movies at once. (This corrects a run-on sentence error.)

Remember that run-on errors can be corrected in four different ways.

Set #50, page 186

1. A world-famous architect designed that church. (Change to active voice.)

2. I served my homemade brownies, baked to absolute perfection. (Place the modifier next to the word it modifies.)

3. Dana and Jeff visited the apartment that they had just bought on Warren Street. (Place the modifier next to the word it modifies.)

4. William Trevor has written many wonderful novels. (Avoid *there are* construction.)

5. Lenny likes rap more than Stephanie does. (Include the second verb to clarify the comparison.)

6. Because Terrence refused to fight, Brandon believed incorrectly that Terrence was a weakling and coward. When he spread around the school that this was so, even Terrence heard the rumor and decided to put Brandon in his place. (Create two shorter sentences instead of one long, confusing one.)

Set #51, page 193

Answers will vary. Here is one model response:

Sometimes it takes an unusual speaker to deliver a much-needed message. (opening sentence) In Carl Sandburg's poem "Grass," the grass that covers battlefields delivers a powerful message: humanity seems to have a hard time learning the lessons of war. (topic sentence, followed by supporting details, including a quote) In the poem, "grass" speaks of five battles from three different eras. Two are from Napoleon's day, one is our Civil War's Battle of Gettysburg, and the last two are from World War I. In each case, however, grass's request is the same: let's bury the bodies and let him do his work. It may take time, but eventually passersby will fail to recognize these locations as places where large numbers of people died. They will "ask the conductor:/ What place is this?/ Where are we now?" According to the narrator, the proof lies in the fact that people keep going to war, and people—lots of them, unfortunately—keep dying. The poet is trying to say that it doesn't take much for people to forget how awful war can be. All it takes is simply letting the grass grow over the battlefield sites.

CHAPTER EIGHT

Putting It All Together: The Research Paper

When you first learn that your teacher is about to assign a research project, your immediate reaction probably is not "Oh, great!" Research projects sound like a lot of work—and they are—but they're interesting, too, for a couple of reasons. First, you get to learn a lot about a topic that may interest you. Second, you get to put into practice many of the skills you've already begun to master.

In fact, take a look at the seven chapters you've already read. Chapter 6, which addresses studying for tests and quizzes, is probably the only chapter that does not apply to the task of creating a research project. The others certainly do. You certainly will need to use your time well and wisely, do some work at home, read various materials, take notes, create outlines, and, finally, write well. If you can do all those tasks well, you will not only be able to write a good research paper; you will be well on your way to becoming a better student.

BRAIN TICKLER
Set #52

Throughout your educational career, you have undoubtedly participated in numerous research projects. Which ones can you recall? Of those, which were your favorites? Why? Which did you enjoy least? Why?

SELECTING A TOPIC

Here's a rule of thumb: the higher your education, the less guidance you will receive in choosing your research topics. One day, should you be lucky enough to pursue advanced degrees, you may experience nearly complete autonomy. That kind of freedom can be a little scary.

The flip side of that coin is that, if you're just starting out in the research biz, you're probably going to get lots of help in selecting a topic. That's excellent news because you don't want to find yourself in a situation in which you've chosen a topic that's either too big or too small. That kind of misstep could result in lost time and perhaps a poor grade.

What makes a topic too big or too small? To understand the answer to that question, you might want to look at a continuum of topics. Here's a range of topics, starting with way too big and ending with a little too small.

- Literature of the twentieth century
- Poetry of the twentieth century
- Poetry of Robert Frost
- The theme of fellowship in Robert Frost's poems
- The early poems of Robert Frost
- The poems of *A Boy's Will* (Frost's first published book of poems)
- Fellowship in "The Tuft of Flowers" (a poem from *A Boy's Will*)
- The impact of Frost's personal experiences on "The Tuft of Flowers"
- Metaphors in "The Tuft of Flowers"

You can see that these topics range from the exceedingly general to the very specific. It ought to be obvious to you that the first topic is huge. You could fill a bookcase with books on that topic (if you could write them). On the other extreme, you might have a hard time writing more than a paragraph on the last question.

Now, if a paragraph is all you have to write, then "Metaphors in 'The Tuft of Flowers'" might be your research project. The point is simply that you need to match a topic to your assignment requirements.

Here are some strategies for doing just that:

1. Try to choose a topic with which you are already familiar. Your store of knowledge on a particular subject will help guide you toward the right sized topic.

2. Ask an expert. Approach your librarian or your teacher and say, "I would like to do a five-page paper on military strategy at the Battle of Gettysburg. Will I have trouble finding enough information on that topic?"

3. Refine your topic as you go along. This is key. Let's say you want to do a paper on recent developments in the prevention of disease. Once you got started on that topic, you would encounter tidal waves of information. "Recent Developments in the Prevention of Kidney Disease" might be more manageable.

Major Mistake Territory!

Given an assignment of this size, don't dawdle. You need to begin promptly. By doing so, you can quickly determine whether your topic is too big or too small, and you can refine it—or change it altogether—as you check out possible sources of information.

Remember: a topic that's too broad will yield an impossibly shallow paper, and a topic that's too narrow will yield an improbably brief one. Either way, your grade goes south.

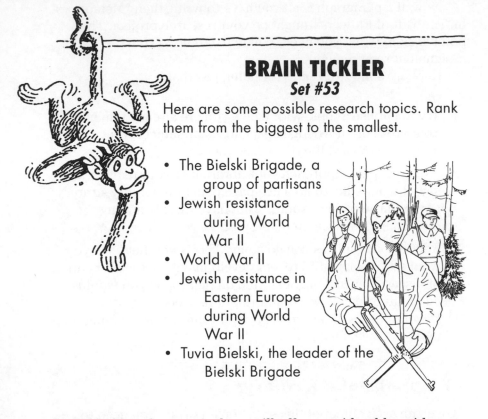

BRAIN TICKLER
Set #53

Here are some possible research topics. Rank them from the biggest to the smallest.

- The Bielski Brigade, a group of partisans
- Jewish resistance during World War II
- World War II
- Jewish resistance in Eastern Europe during World War II
- Tuvia Bielski, the leader of the Bielski Brigade

In all likelihood, your teachers will offer considerable guidance in helping you choose a topic. This is especially true as you're starting out in the realm of independent research. Your teacher may ask you to select a topic from a list of acceptable and manageable subjects. In fact, it's quite possible that your teacher will assign a specific topic to you. Because teachers are a caring and attentive bunch, yours will probably attempt to pair your skills and interests with a suitable topic. (You can always hope!)

MAKING A SCHEDULE

Completing a research project is a significant undertaking, one that consists of varied tasks and requires a considerable amount of time. It's not something you can save for the last minute—not if you wish to do well and not if you wish to get anything out of it.

Therefore, you need to create a schedule. Now, chances are your teacher will give you some assistance with this, especially if many or all of the tasks are to be completed in school. In any case, you need to think of your project's components:

1. Choosing a topic
2. Conducting the research—This includes locating and reading sources and writing note cards and source cards. It also involves determining whether you have enough information.
3. Creating an outline
4. Writing a first draft
5. Writing a final draft
6. Creating a Works Cited page

In planning your schedule, you need to take into account lots of different factors:

- How much of the work will be done in school? How much will you need to complete on your own time?
- How long is the assignment? Obviously, a ten-page paper will require much more time than will a three-page requirement.
- How familiar are you with the subject?
- How difficult is the material you must read?

- What kind of stamina do you possess? Let's face it: some students can work for hours, whereas others can work in increments of thirty minutes. You know your own capabilities.
- What other commitments and requirements (tests, sports, work, etc.) could interfere with your schedule.

When all is said and done, keep in mind this rule of thumb: allocate as much time to research (steps 1–2) as to pre-writing and writing (steps 3–4).

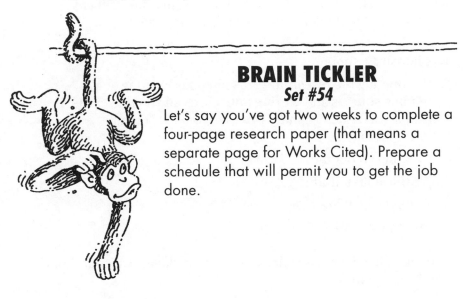

BRAIN TICKLER
Set #54

Let's say you've got two weeks to complete a four-page research paper (that means a separate page for Works Cited). Prepare a schedule that will permit you to get the job done.

Picture this scenario. In your English class, you are reading Tony Earley's novel, *Jim the Boy*, which is set in rural North Carolina in the 1930s. In your social studies class, you are about to embark upon a unit on the Great Depression. In your health class, your teacher has been studying diseases. These three teachers put their heads together and decide to create a research project that will combine their disciplines and your academic needs.

They create a list of five research topics:

1. Ty Cobb and Baseball in the 1930s (Cobb makes a cameo appearance in the novel, and baseball plays an important part in the lives of the characters.)
2. The Effect of the Great Depression on Family Life
3. The Issue of Race in the 1930s (A minor character in the novel must confront bigotry.)
4. Producing and Selling Alcohol Illegally during Prohibition (An important character in the novel goes to prison for doing just this.)
5. Polio in the 1930s (An important character in the novel is suddenly afflicted with polio.)

Your task is to write a newspaper article of two to three pages on the topic of your choosing. Your English teacher has explained the difference between a hard news (late-breaking) article and a feature story. In any case, you understand that you will be writing your piece as if you were alive back in the 1930s. You also must compile note cards containing at least twenty-five notes (each bulleted item is considered a separate note) taken from at least three different sources, one of which must be a book. In addition, you must submit a Works Cited page.

Because you're interested in science and health and because you do well in both subjects, let us assume that the topic you select is "Polio in the 1930s."

You don't know much about polio, except that it's a disease of some kind that affects the central nervous system. You know that polio used to be a major medical problem, but for some reason you hardly hear of it nowadays. You certainly do not know anyone who has ever had it.

With that in mind, where should you begin?

FINDING THE BEST SOURCES

An encyclopedia can be an excellent place to start. A good encyclopedia entry will give you a broad overview of a topic. You'll be able to take many useful notes, and you'll often obtain a very good sense of where you need to go next.

Major Mistake Territory!

Beware of online encyclopedias! Some online encyclopedias permit readers to "update" entries. The result of a policy of this nature is that you cannot depend on an article's factual accuracy.

Do you want to know which encyclopedias (book form, CD-rom, or online) are best? Ask your librarian.

Librarians love to be helpful. They possess a huge fund of knowledge, and they are eager to share their expertise with researchers. Your librarian is a great person for you to get to know.

If you look up "Polio" in the "P" section of *The Classic Encyclopedia*, a glance will tell you that this entry will provide exactly what you want, a general overview of the topic. So your next step will be to prepare a source card.

1

Anderson, Nicholas. "Poliomyelitis." *The Classic Encyclopedia*. 2006 edition.

You will remember that the number in the corner indicates that this is the first source you consulted. Every note card based on this source will also contain this number.

As you read the entry, you decide to compile the following note cards.

1

Poliomyelitis

- also called polio and infantile paralysis
- epidemics common before 1950s
- disease greatly feared

1

Different Kinds

- mild form—fever, headache, sore throat, vomiting; may disappear after day
- severe form—same symptoms do not disappear; also pain in neck and back and muscle weakness; paralysis may develop
- spinal poliomyelitis—most common form; attacks nerve cells of muscles, incl diaphragm (breathing)
- bulbar paralysis—most serious form damages cells of brain stem; affects swallowing, breathing, circulation
- post-polio syndrome—sometimes symptoms return, as late as 30 yrs

---

1

Causes

- viruses enter body through nose & mouth
- enter nerve cell and multiply so rapidly that cell is damaged or destroyed
- paralysis results when lots of cells are lost
- having virus does not mean you will get polio

1

Prevention

- Salk vaccine (injection)—1955
- Sabin vaccine (oral)—1961
- children vaccinated early and often

1

Treatment

- no cure
- immediate medical care, good nursing affect chances of recovery
- complete rest necessary
- physical therapy
- some need splints, braces, or crutches
- if breathing muscles are paralyzed, some kind of respirator is used

Pretty good so far, right? Well, that's not all. At the end of the article, you come across a section entitled, "Related Articles in *The Classic Encyclopedia*." In this section you find the name of Franklin D. Roosevelt, and a light goes off in your ample brain. You remember two things: Roosevelt had polio, and he was also America's president during the period you're studying.

BRAIN TICKLER
Set #55

You want to get more information about President Roosevelt and polio. Having already availed yourself of a book (in this case, an encyclopedia), you decide to check out some online sources. What's your strategy for finding some really good information on this topic?

Many sites will provide excellent information about President Roosevelt and his bout with polio.

Again, your first step would be to prepare a source card.

2

"President Roosevelt and Polio." *The President Roosevelt Website.* http://www.fdr/polio (5 March 2008).

Once again, notice the numeral "2" in the upper right-hand corner. This means that every note from this source will also bear that numeral.

After carefully reading this website, you construct the following note cards:

2

Onset of Illness

- August 10, 1921, when FDR was 39
- on vacation at Campobello Island, New Bruns.—sailing, resting, jogging, swimming
- overcome by exhaustion
- fever of 102 next morning
- fatigue in legs, pain in neck and back
- by next night, cannot move legs

2

Initial Diagnosis

- family doctor unable to diagnose at first
- when symptoms fail to improve, specialist tells FDR he has polio
- Sept.: family returns to NY
- after some months of improvement in neck & back, docs tell FDR that paralysis of legs is permanent

2

Early Treatment

- FDR refuses to accept diagnosis
- 7 yrs of daily exercise and PT
- practices walking with crutches, heavy leg braces
- looks in vain for "cures" (incl. electric currents, mineral baths), and would continue to do so for whole life

2

FDR and Warm Springs

- 1924—FDR 1st learns that waters helped another polio victim to walk again
- he, too, enjoyed waters and warm Georgia sun
- FDR bought the resort => Georgia Warm Springs Foundation (1927)
- quits daily involvement w/ Foundation when he decides to run for NYS Gov.

2

The Campaign for Governor (1928)

- cannot be seen as a "cripple"—stereotype: person w/ physical disability also had mental/emotional flaws
- traveled in back seat of open car—iron bar so he can stand easily
- used sarcasm about his being an "unfortunate sick man"
- addressed audience standing
- used aides effectively for support so he didn't appear to struggle
- "gentleman's agreement" w/ press: not photographed in vulnerable positions (e.g., in wheelchair)

2

FDR as President

- as Pres (elected 1932), FDR doesn't have to move about so much—can work mostly from White House
- uses secret service to help w/ public appearance (e.g., to build ramps and attach podium to floor)
- maintained very busy schedule, laying to rest fears that his disability would limit him (e.g., in 1st 100 days, passed New Deal legislation)

BRAIN TICKLER
Set #56

OK, the ball's in your court! Find a third source—either printed or electronic—and get some additional information about FDR and polio. Specifically, you want to find out how FDR served as an advocate (supporter) of people with disabilities. Prepare a source card and note cards.

You have now completed your research. You have in front of you about fifteen note cards, each containing anywhere from one to a half-dozen notes. In other words, you have plenty of information. What's your next step?

Major Mistake Territory!

You may *think* you have completed your research. Maybe you actually have. But you need to keep your mind open to the possibility that your research is not fully done.

As you're creating an outline or, later, doing the actual writing, you may discover that you have some gaps in your work. You have a story you need to tell, but you don't have all the information you need to tell it.

Don't be frustrated. This happens to writers and researchers all the time. Having come this far, you know where to find the information you need, so just go for it.

CREATING AN OUTLINE

Ever mindful of your assignment, you know that you must write an article. You know that an article is based on a specific event. A good writer provides information pertaining to that event and also uses this article to give the reader all the background he or she requires.

That brings you to your next big question. Upon which specific event will you base your article?

You go back to the original assignment: your teacher wants you to write an article *as if you were living in the 1930s*. That narrows things down a bit.

BRAIN TICKLER
Set #57

So, in order to select that one specific event, you look through your note cards yet again. Create a list of events that you might select.

Having narrowed your choices to three, you decide to go with the first: Nation's First Disabled President Adapts to Physical Demands of His Office (1933). Even though this particular topic does not focus upon a late-breaking news event, you recognize that it is the topic for which you are best prepared. It is the topic for which you already have the most information.

So what shape will your article take?

First, you'll need a title (the one above should do the trick), and you also need a dateline. If FDR took office in January of 1933 and you wish to write about his first 100 days in office, why not use, say, May 15, 1933 as your dateline?

All articles begin with a lead, and yours will follow directly from the title. That's easy enough. You might create something that will look this:

Nation's First Disabled President Adapts to Physical Demands of His Office

May 15, 1933. President Franklin Delano Roosevelt, the thirty-second man to occupy the nation's highest office, faces a challenge unique to his position: he is a victim of poliomyelitis. But, judging by his first 100 days in office, this particular "victim" is not about to let this disability get the best of him.

Looks pretty good so far, right? Well, that's the easy part, actually.

Now you need to think about organizing the body of the article. You know that the body of a news story is sometimes called an inverted pyramid because it begins with the most important information and ends with the least important.

So what's most important? That's easy. You need to answer this question: *how* has FDR adjusted to the demands of his office? You already have the answer: just look at the note card entitled "FDR as President."

And there's the first part of your outline:

I. FDR's adjustment as Pres.

   A. as Pres (elected 1932), FDR doesn't have to move about so much—can work mostly from White House

   B. uses secret service to help w/ public appearance (e.g., to build ramps and attach podium to floor)

   C. maintained very busy schedule, laying to rest fears that his disability would limit him (e.g., in 1st 100 days, passed New Deal legislation)

Well done! It makes good sense to begin your story this way, with the most recent and most important pieces of news.

But what comes next?

You have two major chunks of information that you ought to present.

The readers of your article will probably want to know something about Roosevelt's illness. When did he first become ill? How severe is his particular case? How has the illness affected him so far?

Also, your readers will probably require some background information about polio. What causes the illness? What are some of its symptoms? What kind of treatment is available?

You have a decision to make: which of these two major chunks of information is more important?

Probably information pertaining to Roosevelt's illness is more important. Why? Because this article is about him, and readers will want to know specific information about his life.

With that in mind, your next challenge is to create an outline for this section of the article. The good news is that you have a great deal of information on this topic.

After looking through your note cards, you might produce an outline that looks like this:

II. History of FDR's illness

   A. Onset of Illness

      1. August 10, 1921, when FDR was 39

      2. on vacation at Campobello Island, New Bruns.— sailing, resting, jogging, swimming

      3. overcome by exhaustion

      4. fever of 102 next morning

      5. fatigue in legs, pain in neck and back

      6. by next night, cannot move legs

  B. Initial Diagnosis

      1. family doctor unable to diagnose at first

      2. when symptoms fail to improve, specialist tells FDR he has polio

      3. Sept.: family returns to NY

      4. after some months of improvement in neck & back, docs tell FDR that paralysis of legs is permanent

  C. Early Treatment

      1. FDR refuses to accept diagnosis

      2. 7 yrs of daily exercise and PT

      3. practices walking with crutches, heavy leg braces

      4. looks in vain for "cures" (incl. electric currents, mineral baths), and would continue to do so for whole life

  D. The Campaign for Governor (1928)

      1. cannot be seen as a "cripple"—stereotype: person w/ physical disability also had mental/emotional flaws

      2. traveled in back seat of open car—iron bar so he can stand easily

      3. used sarcasm about his being an "unfortunate sick man"

      4. addressed audience standing

      5. used aides effectively for support so he didn't appear to struggle

      6. "gentleman's agreement" w/ press: not photographed in vulnerable positions (e.g., in wheelchair)

This is starting to look like one very impressive article, right?

BRAIN TICKLER
Set #58

Go back to the first set of notes on polio, taken from the *Classic Encyclopedia*. Determine which of these notes would be suitable for the article on President Roosevelt. Create an outline based on these notes.

With an outline of this length and detail, you will have no trouble writing an article of two pages. In fact, you'll probably have to leave something out! In any case, even this "shared" research experience should prove a valuable point: if you research carefully and correctly, and if you create a full, sensible outline, the writing will pretty much take care of itself.

This book will neither ask you to write the actual article, nor will it present you with a finished one. However, one relatively simple task does await you: you must prepare a Works Cited page.

THE WORKS CITED PAGE

The purpose of a Works Cited page is to give your reader a chance to consult the same sources that you used in your research. (The Works Cited page used to be called a bibliography. Some may continue to call it that. The main difference between the two is that the Works Cited page lists those sources you actually used in your writing, whereas a bibliography lists every source you consulted.) A reader might wish to double-check your information or maybe get some additional information for himself.

Different style publications require different formats for Works Cited entries. Your teacher will probably make clear to you his or her specific requirements for your Works Cited page. Keep in mind that your source cards already contain all the information your Works Cited page will require. If you have compiled those properly, most of your work is already done.

Nevertheless, some general principles apply:

- Write "Works Cited" on top of the page.
- Entries should be alphabetized by the first word of each entry.
- Entries should be single-spaced. The second line of an entry should be indented five spaces.
- Double-space between entries.
- The title of a magazine, book, or specific web page is italicized (underline if you are writing by hand). The title of an article is surrounded by quotation marks.

Generally, each entry consists of three pieces of information. These are:

- The Author. An author's name is written last name, first name (e.g., Robinson, Marilynne). If a book is written by more than one person, only the first name is presented in this way (e.g., Robinson, Marilynne and Richard Smith).
- The Title. This could refer to the title of an article or the title of a magazine, book, or website. It could refer to both, that is, a specific article contained within some other publication. Include as much information as you can.
- Publication Information. This will vary according to the kind of source you are citing.

Each of these pieces of information is almost like a separate sentence. Use periods to separate them.

Major Mistake Territory!

Who's the author?

Sometimes that question is easier asked than answered. Don't make yourself crazy if you can't find the author's name. Some encyclopedia entries will not list an author. Some articles on websites will not identify an author.

If that's the case, just begin your entry with the title.

Here are some typical Works Cited entries:

- An entry for a book (with a single author):

Goodwin, Doris Kearns. *No Ordinary Time: Franklin and Eleanor Roosevelt: The Home Front in World War II*. New York: Simon & Schuster, 1994.

(Notice the format for publication information: city of publication: name of publisher, date of publication.)

- An entry for an article in an encyclopedia (author *not* identified):

"Developmental Disabilities." *The World Book Encyclopedia*. 2005 ed.

(An encyclopedia entry requires very little publication information: simply the year of the edition will suffice.)

- An entry for an article in a magazine:

Goldstein, Jeffrey. "Investing in Organic Produce." *Business Forecast* 15 Apr. 2007: 33–37.

(Notice that the publication information includes the title of the magazine, its date of publication, and the pages on which the article appears.)

- An interview:

Reagan, Fiona. Personal Interview. 25 Mar. 2006.

- An article from an online website (author identified):

Richardson, Haley. "Choosing the Right Navigation Device." *Getting There.com*. 30 Oct. 2004. http://www.gettingthere.com/travel/navigationdevices.htm (15 Nov. 2005).

(Notice that two dates are given: one for the posting and, later, one for the date the website was visited. The former will not always be available; if it is, you should include it. Again, notice how each part of the entry is treated like a separate sentence with a period at its end. Keep in mind that if the author's name had not been provided, the entry would begin with the title: "Choosing the Right Navigation Device.")

Of course, this is just a sample of five different kinds of entries. There are many more. Make sure you pay attention when your teacher or librarian discusses citation, so that you will know exactly what is required.

BRAIN TICKLER
Set #59

Prepare a Works Cited page for the three sources consulted in this chapter. Two of them are listed within the chapter. (Hint: check the source cards!) The third is the one you contacted on your own when you investigated how FDR served as an advocate for polio and disability.

BRAIN TICKLERS
THE ANSWERS

Set #52, page 203

Answers will vary.

Set #53, page 206

Ranked biggest to smallest:
- World War II
- Jewish resistance during World War II
- Jewish resistance in Eastern Europe during World War II
- The Bielski Brigade, a group of partisans
- Tuvia Bielski, the leader of the Bielski Brigade

Set #54, page 208

Answers will vary. Your schedule could, however, look like this:

- Monday: Select topic.
- Tuesday through Thursday, 3:00 to 3:45: Conduct research in library.
- Friday, 3:00 to 3:45: Review materials, and conduct additional research.
- Sunday: 1:00 to 2:00: Write outline.
- Monday through Wednesday, 3:00 to 3:45: Write first draft.
- Thursday, 3:00 to 4:00: Revise.
- Friday, 3:00 to 4:00: Write Works Cited.

Set #55, page 212

This is easy enough. Choose your search engine, and simply enter keywords "FDR and polio," and you will be presented with a selection of excellent options. Some will offer limited information about the topic; others will address it in great detail. Choose the one that suits your needs.

Set #56, page 215

Your answers will vary. Certainly your source card will depend entirely upon the source you consulted. Notice, however, that these sample note cards all contain the numeral "3" to indicate that this is the third source.

3

- 1941: FDR proposes federal rehab program; despite Congressional opposition, a modified version is passed

3

The March of Dimes

- "Birthday Ball" (1934)—FDR's friend Basil O'Connor holds 1st party to raise funds for treatment of polio
- FDR urges O'Connor to create National Foundation for Infantile Paralysis (March of Dimes is its main fundraising event)
- scientists, with help from public contributions, provide better treatment for victims
- eventually find cure in 1955 (Jonas Salk vaccine)

3

FDR acknowledges his disability

- after Yalta conference with Churchill and Stalin, FDR reports to Congress from his wheelchair

Set #57, page 216

You really don't have that many choices. Your polio cards include very little information about developments in the 1930s and nothing that might furnish a hard news story connected to FDR. Although your FDR cards include lots of specific, hard news-type information, much of that occurs before or after the decade of the 1930s. This leaves you with a few choices:

- Nation's First Disabled President Adapts to Physical Demands of His Office (1933)
- FDR Hosts 1st Birthday Ball (1934)
- The National Foundation for Infantile Paralysis Launches March of Dimes (1938)

Set #58, page 220

Answers will vary. An outline of polio notes could look like this:

III. General Info about Poliomyelitis

    A. also called polio and infantile paralysis

    B. epidemics common before 1950s

    C. disease greatly feared

    D. Causes

        1. viruses enter body through nose & mouth

        2. enter nerve cell and multiply so rapidly that cell is damaged or destroyed

        3. paralysis results when lots of cells are lost

        4. having virus does not mean you will get polio

    E. Different Types

        1. mild form—fever, headache, sore throat, vomiting; may disappear after day

        2. severe form—same symptoms do not disappear; also pain in neck and back and muscle weakness; paralysis may develop

        3. spinal poliomyelitis—most common form; attacks nerve cells of muscles, incl diaphragm (breathing)

        4. bulbar paralysis—most serious form damages cells of brain stem; affects swallowing, breathing, circulation

        5. post-polio syndrome—sometimes symptoms return, as late as 30 yrs

    F. Treatment

        1. no cure

        2. immediate medical care, good nursing affect chances of recovery

        3. complete rest necessary

        4. physical therapy

        5. some need splints, braces, or crutches

        6. if breathing muscles are paralyzed, some kind of respirator is used

Set #59, page 223

Answers will vary, depending upon the third source you consulted. But a Works Cited page for the two already listed would look like this:

Works Cited

Anderson, Nicholas. "Poliomyelitis." *The Classic Encyclopedia*. 2006 ed.
"President Roosevelt and Polio." *The President Roosevelt Web site*. http://www.fdr/polio (5 March 2008).

Acknowledgments

Page 3: excerpt from "To His Coy Mistress," by Andrew Marvell, from *The Case for Poetry*, by Frederick L. Gwynn, Ralph W. Condee, and Arthur O. Lewis, Jr., copyright 1965, by Prentice-Hall, Inc.

Page 35: "Dust of Snow," by Robert Frost, from *Sound and Sense*, by Laurence Perrine and Thomas R. Arp, copyright 1992, by Harcourt Brace Jovanovich.

Page 58: excerpt from *Great Expectations*, by Charles Dickens, copyright 1980, by New American Library.

Page 59: excerpt from "The Necklace," by Guy de Maupassant, from *The Necklace and Other Stories*, copyright 2003, by Dover Publications.

Page 62: excerpt from *Pride and Prejudice*, by Jane Austen, copyright 1956, by the Riverside Press.

Page 63: excerpt from *Treasure Island*, by Robert Louis Stevenson, copyright 1982, by Bantam Classics.

Pages 64–65, 67: "Loveliest of Trees," by A. E. Housman, from *Sound and Sense*, by Laurence Perrine and Thomas R. Arp, copyright 1992, by Harcourt Brace Jovanovich.

Page 66: excerpt from "There's Nothing Like Instinct, Fortunately," by Ogden Nash, from *The World of Poetry*, by Murray Rockowitz and Milton Kaplan, copyright 1965, by Globe Book Company.

Page 68: "Travel," by Edna St. Vincent Millay, from *The World of Poetry*, by Murray Rockowitz and Milton Kaplan, copyright 1965, by Globe Book Company.

Pages 96–99: excerpts from *The Bridge of San Luis Rey*, by Thornton Wilder, copyright 1927, by Avon Books.

Page 116: "Oh, When I Was in Love With You," by A. E. Housman, from *Shropshire Lad*, by A. E. Housman, copyright 1996, by Buccaneer Books.

ACKNOWLEDGMENTS

Page 187: "Richard Cory," by Edwin Arlington Robinson, from *The World of Poetry*, by Murray Rockowitz and Milton Kaplan, copyright 1965, by Globe Book Company.

Page 193: "Grass," by Carl Sandburg, from *The World of Poetry*, by Murray Rockowitz and Milton Kaplan, copyright 1965, by Globe Book Company.

INDEX